COUNTRY QUILTS
for CHILDREN

designs by
Cheryl A. Benner

text by
Rachel T. Pellman

Good Books ®
Intercourse, Pa 17534

Acknowledgments

Design by Cheryl A. Benner
Cover and color photography by
Jonathan Charles

Country Quilts for Children

© 1992 by Good Books,
Intercourse, PA 17534
International Standard Book Number:
1-56148-063-0
Library of Congress Catalog Card Number:
92-16310

Library of Congress Cataloging-in-Publication Data

Benner, Cheryl A., 1962-
    Country quilts for children : featuring Noah's country ark quilt and
    the country circus quilt/Cheryl A. Benner ; text by Rachel T.
    Pellman.

        p.   cm.
    ISBN 1-56148-063-0 (paper) : $12.95
    1. Patchwork—Patterns.   2. Appliqué—Patterns.   3. Children's
quilts.   I. Pellman, Rachel T. (Rachel Thomas)   II. Title.
TT835.B335   1992
746.46—dc20   92-16310
                                                              CIP

Table of Contents

5   Noah's Country Ark Quilt

5   Applique Quilts
5   Preparing Background Fabric for Appliqueing
5   Making Templates
6   Appliqueing
6   Marking Quilt Patches for Piecing
6   Piecing
7   Assembling the Appliqued Quilt Top
7   Quilting on Applique and Pieced Quilts
7   Marking Quilting Designs
7   Quilting
7   Binding
8   To Display Quilts
8   Signing and Dating Quilts
8   Cutting Layout for Noah's Country Ark Quilt
8   Assembly Instructions for Noah's Country Ark
11   Noah's Country Ark Quilt Applique Layout
         (Top, Large Diamond Patch)
25   Noah's Country Ark Quilt Applique Templates
41   Noah's Country Ark Quilt Applique Layout
         (Left Side Triangle Patch)
55   Noah's Country Ark Quilt Applique Templates
73   Noah's Country Ark Quilt Applique Layout
         (Right Side Triangle Patch)
85   Noah's Country Ark Quilt Applique Templates
101   Noah's Country Ark Quilt Applique Layout
         (Large, Bottom Diamond Patch)
125   Noah's Country Ark Quilt Applique Templates
161   Noah's Country Ark Quilt Applique Layout
         (Winding Vine)
165   Noah's Country Ark Quilt Quilting and Piecing Layout

172   The Country Circus Quilt

9   Cutting Layout for The Country Circus Quilt
9   Assembly Instructions for The Country Circus Quilt
173   The Country Circus Quilt Applique Layout
         (Center Diamond Patch)
193   The Country Circus Quilt Applique Templates
209   The Country Circus Quilt Applique Layout
         (Small Patch)
211   The Country Circus Quilt Piecing Templates
213   The Country Circus Quilt Quilting Layout
219   The Country Circus Quilt Quilting Templates
221   The Country Circus Quilt Pieced Border
223   Fabric Requirements
224   About the Old Country Store
224   About the Authors

*F*or years grown-ups have made quilts as gifts of love for children. Many of these quilts are created in anticipation of a new baby. Some are made to commemorate special events. Others are made for "everyday," simply stitched with love to warm not only the body but also the soul.

Country Quilts for Children provides patterns for any parent or grandparent, relative or friend who wants to create a charming and whimsical quilt for a baby or young child.

A crib quilt, because of its less daunting size, is a project suitable for a beginning quiltmaker. The patterns presented here offer enough detail and challenge to capture the imagination of the most adventuresome quilter, also. A wide-mouthed hippo and its bashful mate, two double-humped camels, trumpeting elephants, a proud and brilliant peacock and a throng of other animals—from the common to the unusual—frolic in the sunshine on the Noah's Ark quilt. The Circus quilt sports two jaunty elephants, a seal cavorting with a beach ball and a pair of long necked giraffes.

Designed to fit cribs, these quilts work equally well as wall pieces and could decorate a room, either hanging or covering a crib mattress.

Both the Noah's Ark and the Circus quilts use a combination of piecework and applique. Eyes, hoofs and other animal details are embroidered. The original quilts are done in bright, lively colors. Soft subdued tones would create an equally fascinating menagerie. The finished quilts will certainly be as individual and as interesting as the quiltmakers who make them!

How to Begin

Read the following instructions thoroughly before beginning work on your quilt.

Wash all fabrics before cutting them. This process will both pre-shrink and test them for colorfastness. If the fabric is not colorfast after one washing, repeat the washings until the water remains clear, or replace the cloth with another fabric. If fabrics are wrinkled after washing and drying, iron them before using them.

Fabrics suitable for quilting are generally lightweight, tightly woven cotton and cotton/polyester blends. They should not unravel easily and should not hold excessive wrinkles when squeezed and released. Because of the hours of time required to make a quilt, it is worth investing in high quality fabrics.

Fabric requirements given here are for standard 45″ wide fabric. If you use wide or more narrow fabrics, calculate the variations you will need.

All seams are sewn using ¼″ seam allowances. Measurements given include seam allowances except for applique pieces (see "How to Applique" section).

Applique Quilts
Preparing Background Fabric

When purchasing fabric, it is best to buy the total amount needed from one bolt of fabric. This will assure that all the patches and borders will be the same shade. Dye lots can vary significantly from bolt to bolt of fabric, and those differences are emphasized when placed next to each other in a quilt top.

Label each piece after it is cut. Mark right and wrong sides of fabric as well.

So that you know where to place the applique pieces on the background piece, trace the applique design lightly on the right side of the background fabric before beginning to stitch. Even though the applique pieces will be laid over these markings and stitched in place, it is important to mark these lines as lightly as possible. On square patches center the applique designs on the background sections.

Making Templates

To make templates from pattern pieces printed in this book, use material that will not wear along the edges from repeated tracing. Cardboard is suitable for pieces being traced only a few times. Plastic lids or the sides of plastic cartons work well for templates that will be used repeatedly. Quilt supply shops and art supply stores carry sheets of plastic that work well for template-making.

There are many varieties of fabric-marking pencils or chalk markers available to quilters. Each has its assets. Before using any pencil, pen, or marker, test it on the fabric to be sure it provides a line that is clear and precise. A regular lead pencil will work on many fabrics.

Quiltmaking demands precision. Remember that as you begin marking. First, test the template you have made against the original printed pattern for accuracy. The applique templates are given in their actual size, without seam allowances. Trace them that way. Then trace them on the right side of the fabric, but spaced far enough apart so that you can cut them approximately ¼" outside the marked line. The traced line is the fold line indicating the exact shape of the applique piece. Since these lines will be on the right side of the fabric and will be on the folded edge, markings should be as light as possible.

Each applique piece needs to be traced separately (rather than having the fabric doubled) so the fold line is marked on each one.

Appliqueing

Begin by appliqueing the cut-out fabric pieces, one at a time, over the placement lines drawn onto the background fabric pieces. Be alert to the sequence in which the pieces are applied, so that sections which overlay each other are done in proper order. In cases where a portion of an applique piece is covered by another, the section being covered does not need to be stitched, since it will be held in place by the stitches of the section that overlays it.

Appliqueing is not difficult, but it does require patience and precision. The best applique work has perfectly smooth curves and sharply defined points. To achieve this, stitches must be very small and tight. First, pin the piece being appliqued to the outline on the background piece. Using thread that matches the piece being applied, stitch the piece to the background section, folding the seam allowance under to the traced line on the applique piece. Fold under only a tiny section at a time. Very small pieces may require that the seam allowance be trimmed to less than ¼" so it can be folded under with less bulk.

The applique stitch is a running stitch that goes through the background fabric and emerges to catch only a few threads of the appliqued piece along the folded line. The needle should re-enter the background piece for the next stitch at almost the same place it emerged, creating a stitch so small that it is almost invisible along the edge of the appliqued piece. Stitches on the underside of the background fabric should be ¹⁄₁₆"–⅛" long.

To form sharp points, fold in one side and stitch almost to the end of the point. Fold in the opposite side to form the point and push the excess seam allowance under with the point of the needle. Excess seam allowance may be trimmed to eliminate bulk. Stitch tightly.

To form smooth curves, clip along the curves to the fold line. Fold under while stitching, using the needle to push under the seam allowances.

Pieced Patches
Marking Quilt Patches for Piecing

There are two ways to mark patches—with or without the seam allowance. If marking with the seam allowance, the template is made large enough to include the seam allowance. The template is then traced, and the fabric cut and sewn ¼" inside the cut edge.

When marking without the seam allowance, the template is made the actual size of the finished piece. The cutting is then done ¼" outside the marked line. The marked line thus serves as a sewing guide. The advantage to this method is that each patch has lines, guaranteeing accurate piecing. The disadvantage is that each patch must be marked individually and cut individually. Try both methods and stick with the one that feels most comfortable to you.

Piecing

If the pieces have been cut and marked accurately, piecing the patches is rewarding and fun. Piecing can be done by hand or by machine. Machine piecing is a great deal faster and in many cases makes a stronger seam. However, it is difficult to be as precise with a machine, especially with tiny pieces. When hand piecing, use a tiny running stitch, reinforced occasionally with a backstitch. Be careful to keep the seam taut, but not so tight as to cause puckering.

Whether piecing by hand or by machine, follow assembly instructions so that all patches are built in straight seam units whenever possible. When corners must be set in, stitch either from the outer edge of the patch to the corner (stopping at the seam allowance), pivot, and sew out to the other edge, or start at the corner, sew to one edge, and then return to the corner and sew the other edge. Practice both methods and choose the one you find most easy to execute.

Quilting is often done by outlining pieced patches. Since it is difficult to quilt through the additional thickness created by the seams, seam allowances should be folded away from the edge of the patch where quilting will be done.

Assembling the Appliqued Quilt Top

When all applique work is completed, the patches are ready to be assembled. See the diagrams on pages 8 and 9. Some piecework is required at this point. Most applique work can be done before assembling the quilt top. However, the leaf vine and a few animal touches on the Noah's Ark quilt will need to be completed after assembly.

Quilting on Applique and Pieced Quilts
Marking Quilting Designs

Quilting designs are marked on the surface of the quilt top. You may use the same marker that you used to mark the applique pieces and quilt patches. Again, a lead pencil provides a thin line and, if used with very little pressure, creates markings that are easily seen for quilting, yet do not distract when the quilt is completed. Remember, quilting lines are not covered up by quilting stitches, so the lines should be light or removable.

Patterns for quilting designs are included in this book. Since some spread over several pages, you will need to assemble them before using them.

Quilting

A quilt consists of three layers—the back or underside of the quilt, the batting, and the top, which is the appliqued layer. Quilting stitches follow a decorative pattern, piercing through all three layers of the quilt "sandwich" and holding it together.

Many quilters prefer to stretch their quilts into large quilting frames. These are built so that the finished area of the quilt can be rolled up as work on it progresses. This type of frame allows space for several quilters to work on the same quilt and is used at quilting bees. Smaller hoops can be used to quilt small sections at a time. If you use one of the smaller frames, it is important that you first spread the three layers smoothly and baste them securely to prevent puckering.

The quilting stitch is a simple running stitch. Quilting needles are called "betweens" and are shorter than "sharps," which are regular handsewing needles. The higher the number, the smaller the needle. Many quilters prefer a size 8 or 9 needle.

Quilting is done with a single strand of quilting thread. Knot the thread and insert the needle through the top layer, about one inch away from the point where quilting should emerge on a marked quilting line. Gently tug the knot through the fabric so it is hidden between the layers. Then bring the needle up through the quilt top, going through all layers of the quilt.

Keep one hand under the quilt to feel when the needle has successfully penetrated all layers and to help guide the needle back up to the surface. Your upper hand receives the needle and repeats the process. It is possible to stack as many as five stitches on the needle before pulling the thread through. However, when your work curves, you have smoother results if you stack fewer stitches. Pull the quilting stitches taut but not so tight as to pucker the fabric. When you have used the entire length of thread, reinforce the stitching with a tiny backstitch. Then reinsert the needle in the top layer, push it through for a long stitch, pull it out and clip it.

The goal in quilting is to have straight, even stitches that are of equal length on both the top and bottom of the quilt. That achievement comes with hours of practice.

When you quilt the applique patches, simply outline the applique designs. This outline quilting will accent the applique section and cause it to appear slightly puffed.

Binding

The final stage in completing a quilt is the binding, which finishes the quilt's raw edge.

A double thickness of binding on the edge of the quilt gives it additional strength and durability. To create a double binding, cut the binding strips 2–2½" wide. Sew strips together to form a continuous length of binding.

Baste the raw edges of the quilt together. Using a ¼" seam allowance, sew the binding along the edge. Trim excess batting and backing to ¼". Wrap the binding around to the back, enclosing the raw edges and covering the stitch line. Slipstitch in place with thread that matches the color of the binding fabric.

To Display Quilts

Wall quilts can be hung in various ways. You can simply tack the quilt directly to the wall. However, this is potentially damaging to both the quilt and wall. Except for a permanent hanging, this is probably not the best way.

Another option is to hang the quilt like a painting. To do this, make a narrow sleeve from matching fabric and handsew it to the upper edge of the quilt along the back. Insert a dowel rod through the sleeve and hang the rod by wire or nylon string.

The quilt can also be hung on a frame. This method requires velcro or fabric to be attached to the frame itself. If you choose velcro, staple one side to the frame. Handsew the opposite velcro on the edge of the quilt, then attach the quilt carefully to the velcro on the frame. If you attach fabric to the frame, handstitch the quilt to the frame itself.

Quilts can also be mounted inside plexiglas by a professional framer. This method, often reserved for antique quilts, can provide an acid-free, dirt free and, with special plexiglas, a sun-proof environment for your quilt.

Signing and Dating Quilts

To preserve history for future generations, sign and date the quilts you make. Include your initials and the year the quilt was made. This date is usually added discreetly in a corner of the quilt. It can be embroidered or quilted among the quilting designs. Another alternative is to stitch or write the information on a separate piece of fabric and handstitch it to the back of the quilt. Whatever method you choose, this is an important part of finishing a quilt.

Noah's Country Ark Quilt
Cutting Layout for Crib Quilt

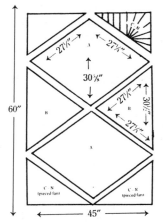

*A Diamonds – cut 1 blue and 1 tan diamond
*B Triangles – cut 2 tan triangles
C through N - Pieced Corner Fan – templates given

*Note: Diagonal edges of diamond and triangle
patches may stretch out of shape
from handling during the applique
process. To avoid this, mark
triangle onto background piece, but
do not cut angled edges until
applique is complete.

Final size — 45" x 60"
Measurements include
seam allowances

Assembly Instructions for
Noah's Country Ark Quilt

1.
2. =
3. =

4. C through N

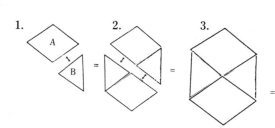

(Assembly of
Pieced Corner fan)

5. =
6. =

Applique sun over pieced
rays above Ark. The
lower edge of the sun
does not need to be
appliqued. It will be
sewn into the seam
when the top is attached
to the main portion of the
quilt.

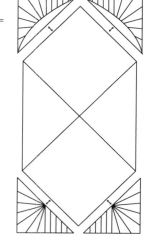

7. Applique leaves and any additional pieces
extending over seams.

The Country Circus Quilt
Cutting Layout for Crib Quilt

Fan – templates given
A – cut 1 – 26½" square
B – cut 4 – 13½" square
C – cut 6 – triangles

D – cut 4 – triangles

E – cut 4 – 3½" squares
F – Pieced Square – template given
G – Pieced Triangle – template given
H – Pieced Triangle – template given

Final size — 45" x 62"
Measurements include
seam allowances

Assembly Instructions for
The Country Circus Quilt

Position Fans in corners of B patches. Baste along straight edges. Applique curved edge of fan to patch turning under ¼ inch seam allowance. Side edges of fan will be secured in seams when patches are sewn together.

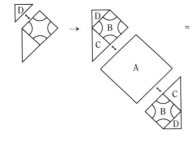

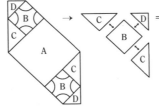

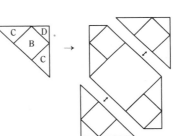

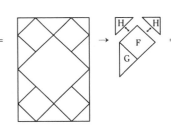

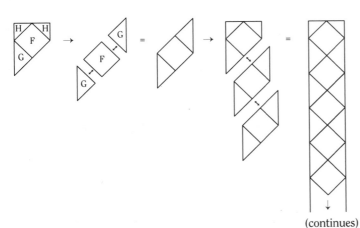

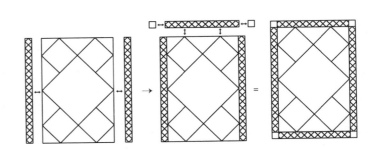

(continues)

Noah's Country Ark Quilt Applique Layout
Top, Large Diamond Patch

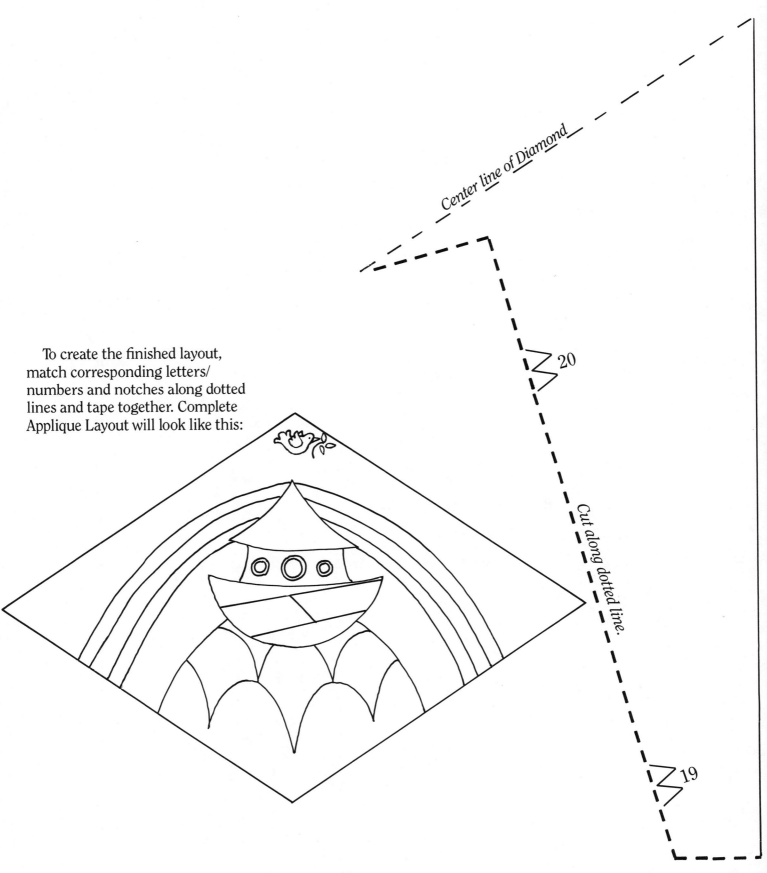

Center line of Diamond

20

Cut along dotted line.

19

To create the finished layout, match corresponding letters/ numbers and notches along dotted lines and tape together. Complete Applique Layout will look like this:

Noah's Country Ark Quilt Applique Layout
Top, Large Diamond Patch

Center line of Diamond

Edge of Diamond Patch

9

8

10

11

Cut along dotted line.

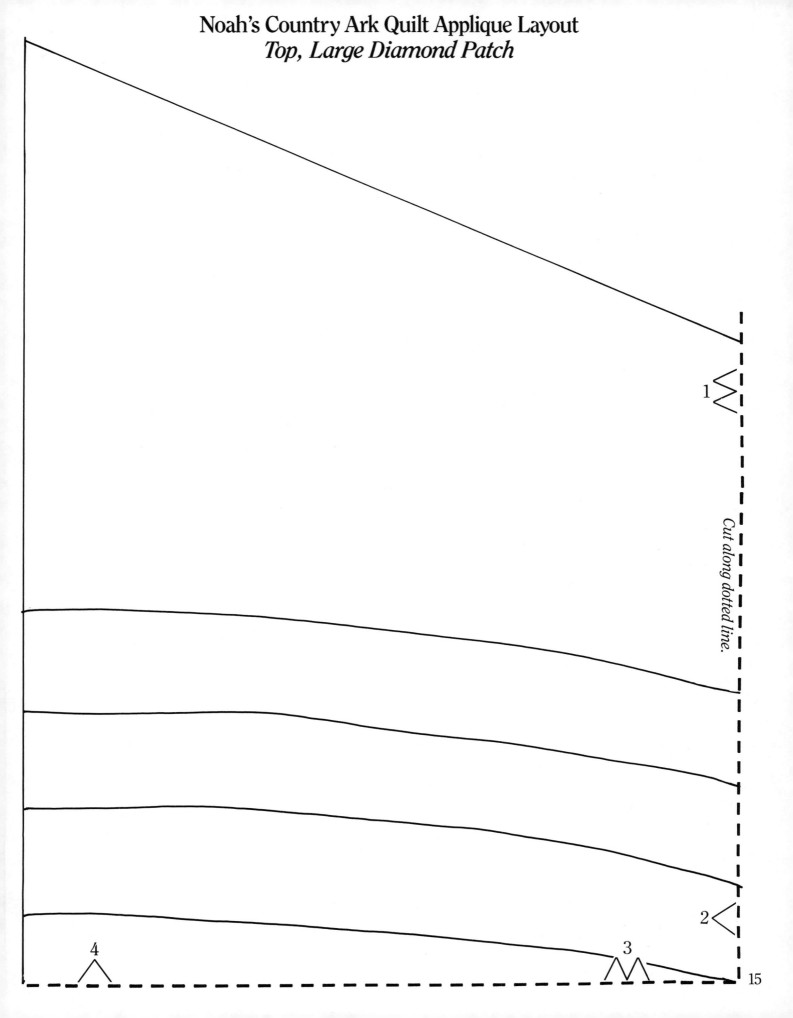

Noah's Country Ark Quilt Applique Layout
Top, Large Diamond Patch

1

2

3

4

Cut along dotted line.

15

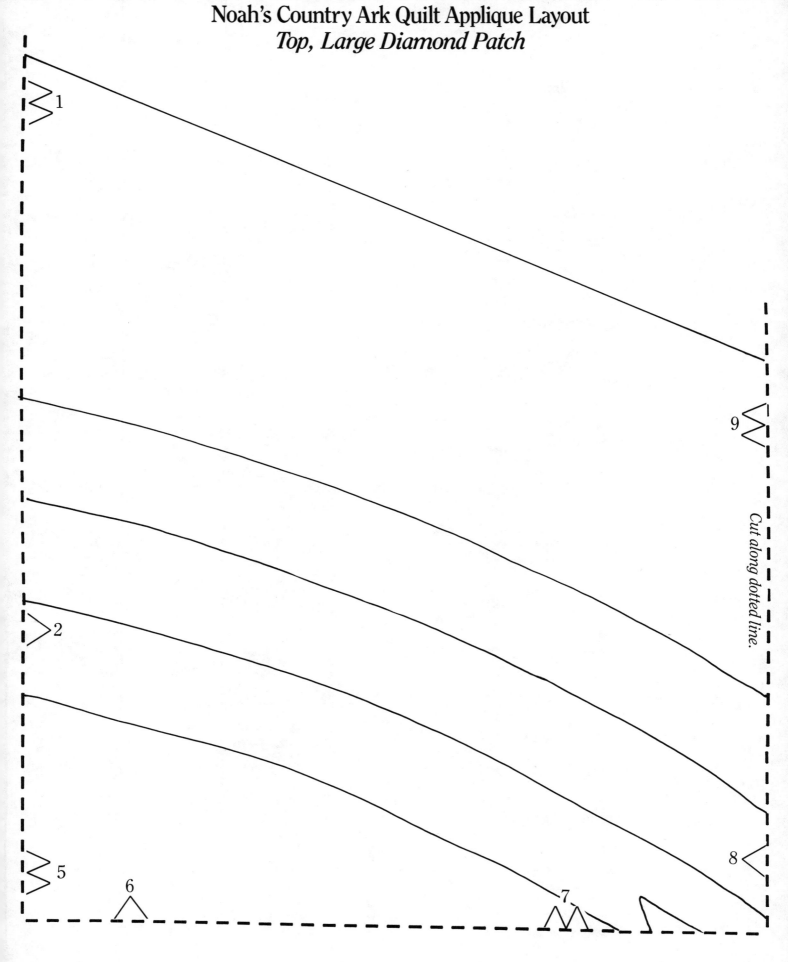

Noah's Country Ark Quilt Applique Layout
Top, Large Diamond Patch

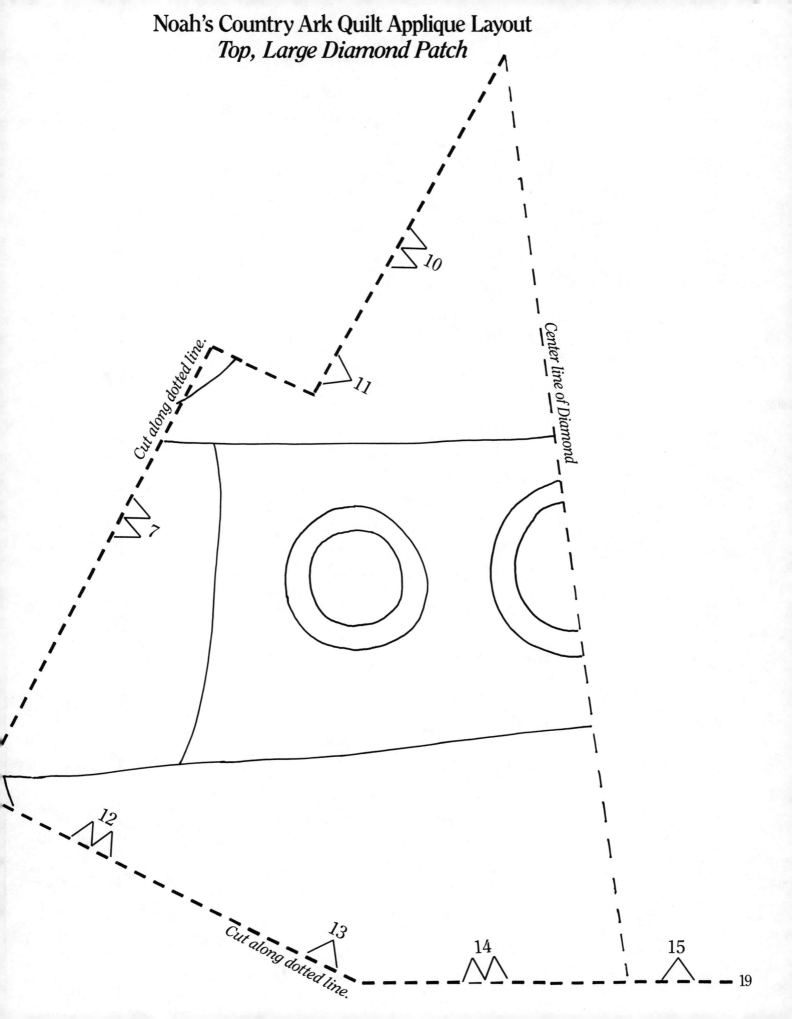

10

11

Center line of Diamond

Cut along dotted line.

7

12

13

Cut along dotted line.

14

15

19

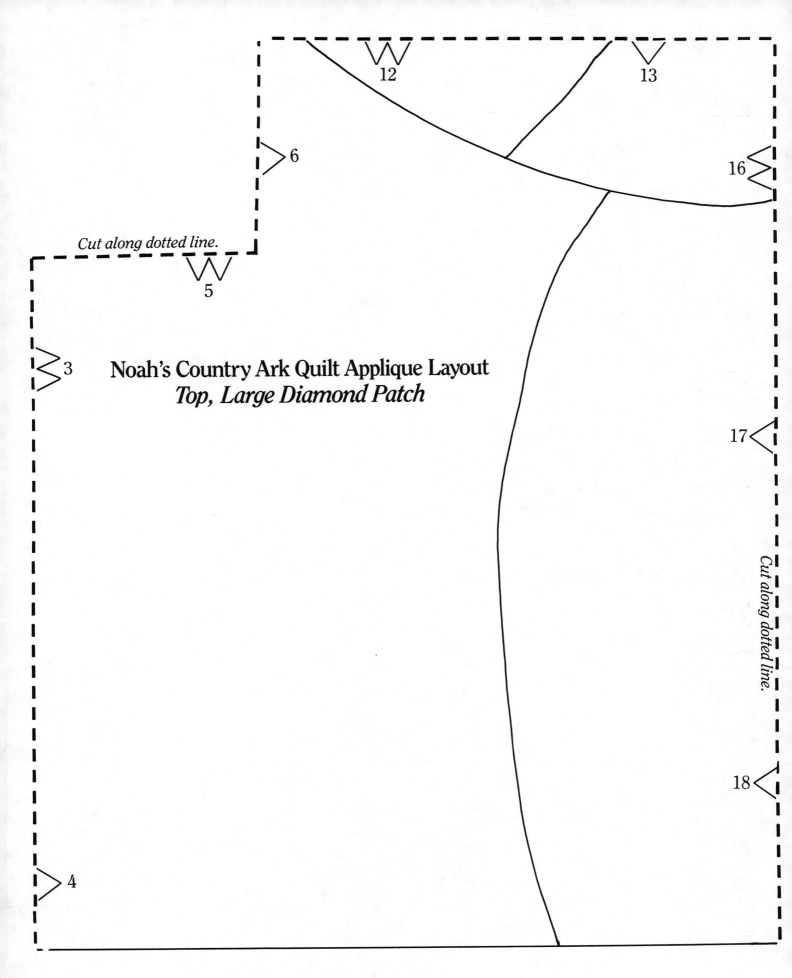

Noah's Country Ark Quilt Applique Layout
Top, Large Diamond Patch

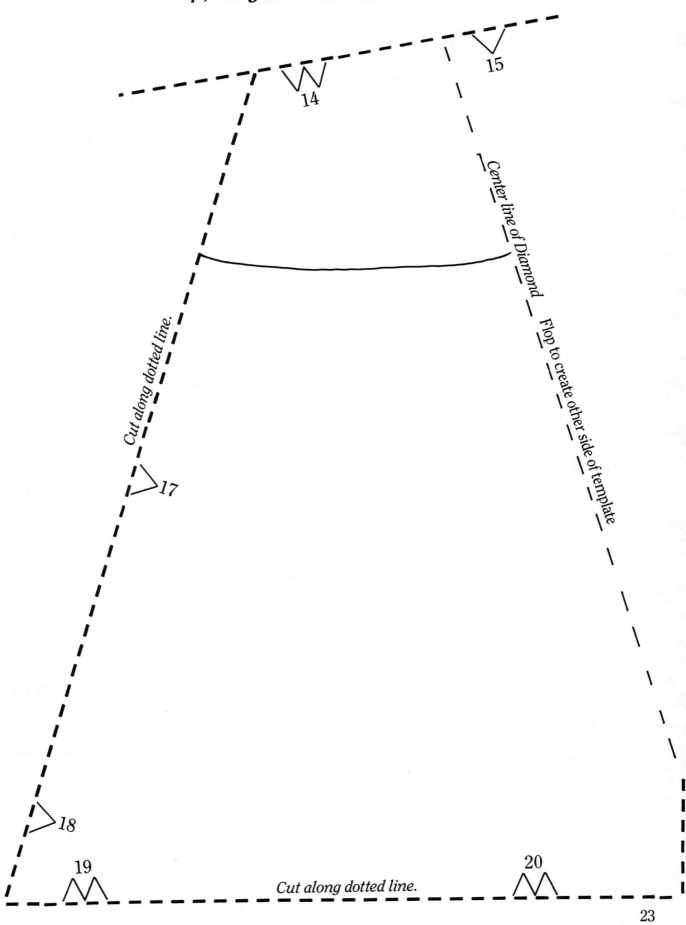

14

15

Center line of Diamond

Flop to create other side of template

Cut along dotted line.

17

18

19

20

Cut along dotted line.

Noah's Country Ark Quilt Applique Templates
Top, Large Diamond Patch

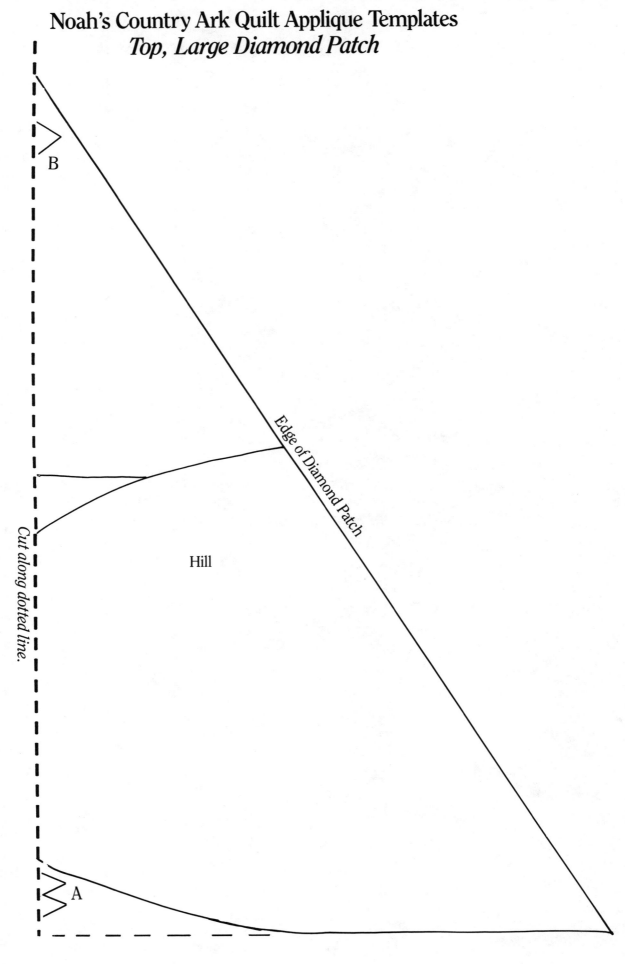

B

Edge of Diamond Patch

Cut along dotted line.

Hill

A

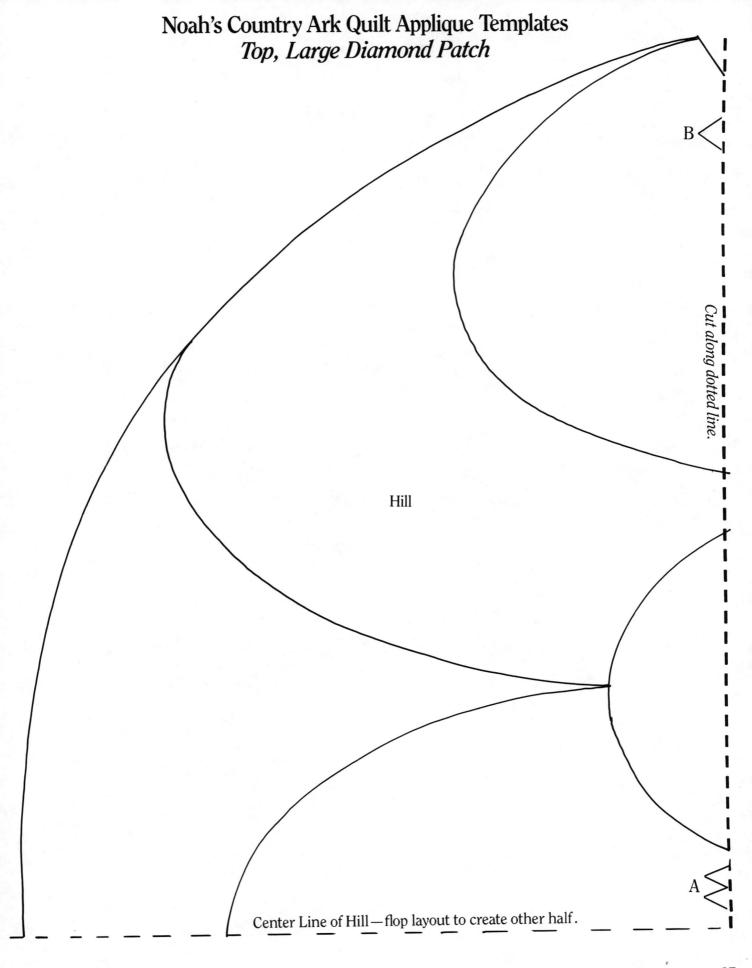

B

Cut along dotted line.

Hill

A

Center Line of Hill—flop layout to create other half.

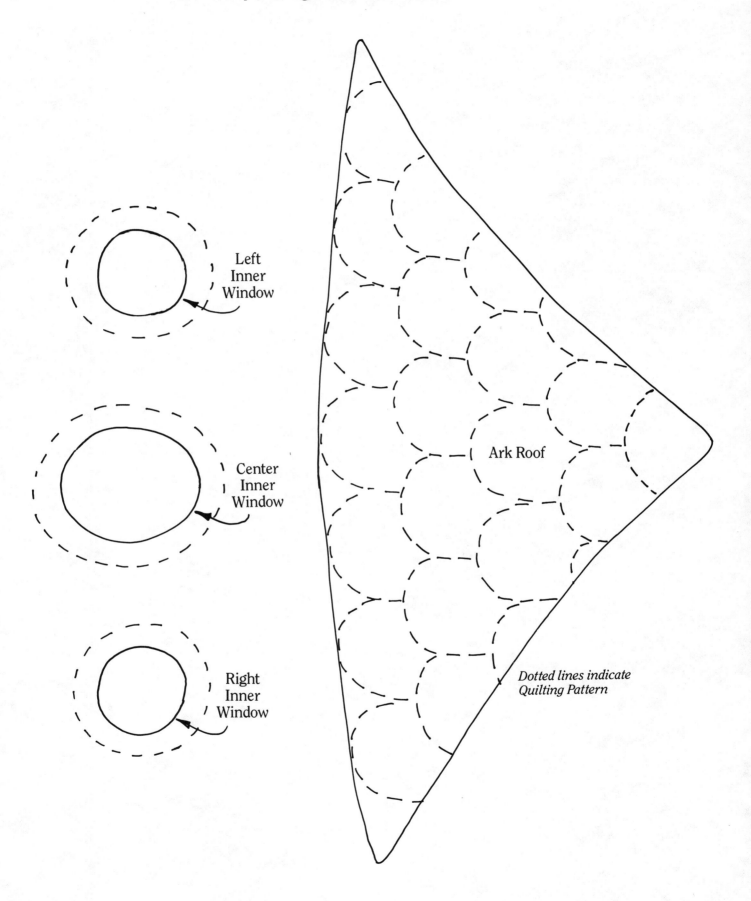

Left
Inner
Window

Center
Inner
Window

Right
Inner
Window

Ark Roof

*Dotted lines indicate
Quilting Pattern*

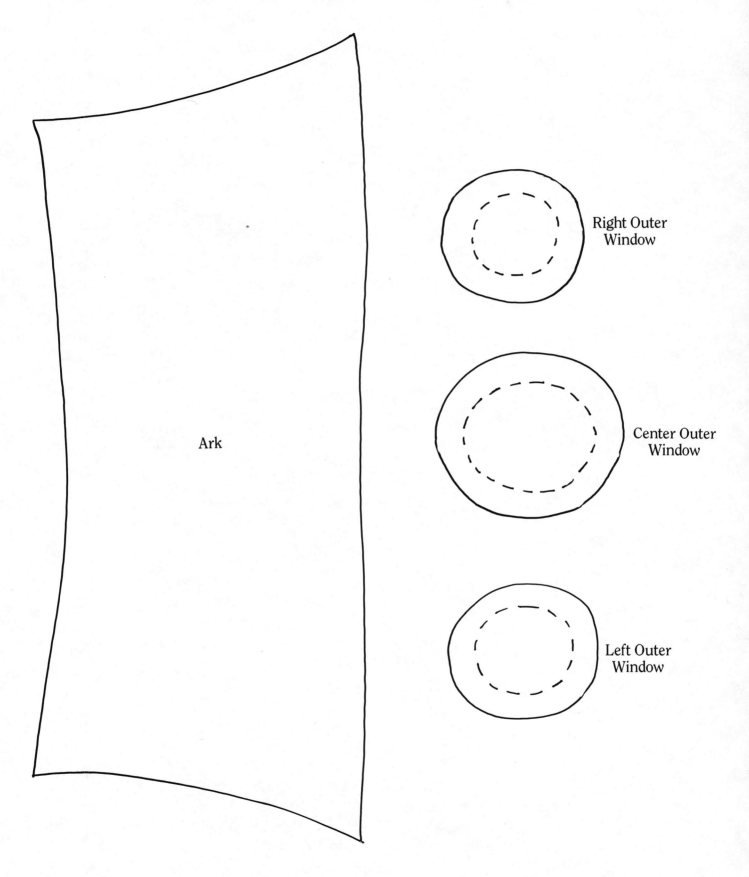

Ark

Right Outer
Window

Center Outer
Window

Left Outer
Window

Noah's Country Ark Quilt Applique Templates
Top, Large Diamond Patch

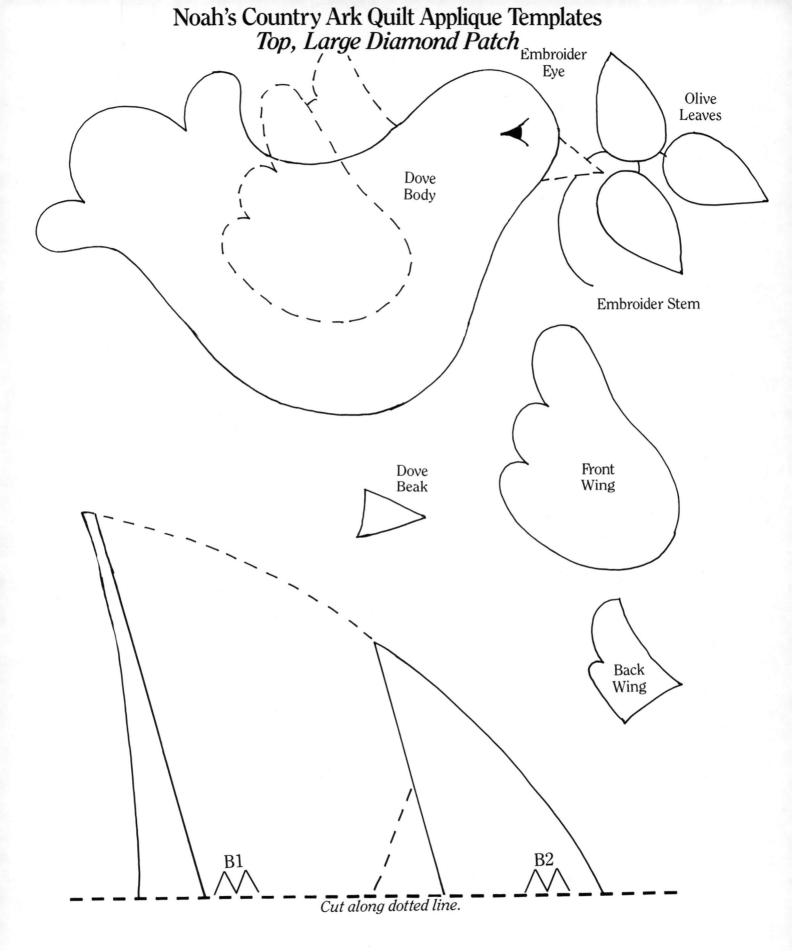

Embroider Eye

Olive Leaves

Dove Body

Embroider Stem

Dove Beak

Front Wing

Back Wing

B1

B2

Cut along dotted line.

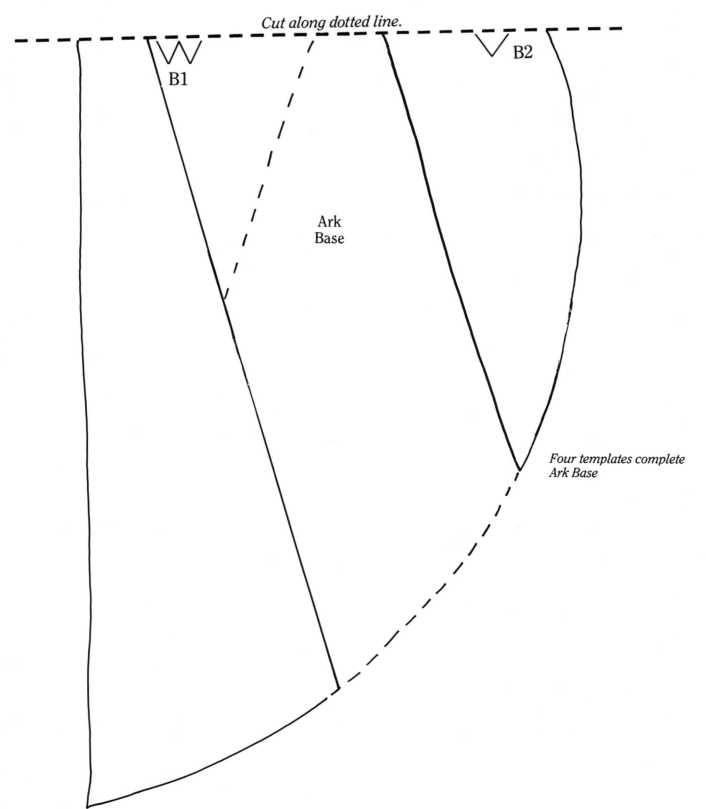

Cut along dotted line.

B1

B2

Ark
Base

*Four templates complete
Ark Base*

Noah's Country Ark Quilt Applique Templates
Top, Large Diamond Patch
Rainbow

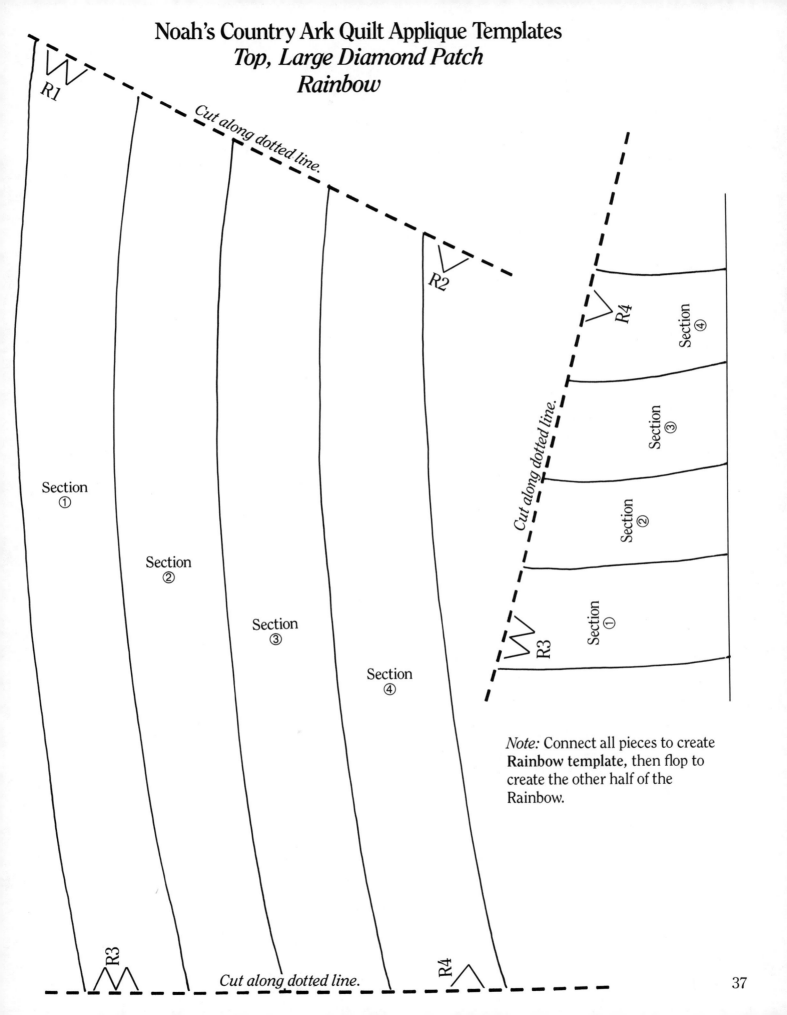

Cut along dotted line.

R1

R2

Section ①

Section ②

Section ③

Section ④

R4

Section ④

Section ③

Section ②

Section ①

R3

Cut along dotted line.

Note: Connect all pieces to create **Rainbow template**, then flop to create the other half of the Rainbow.

R3

R4

Cut along dotted line.

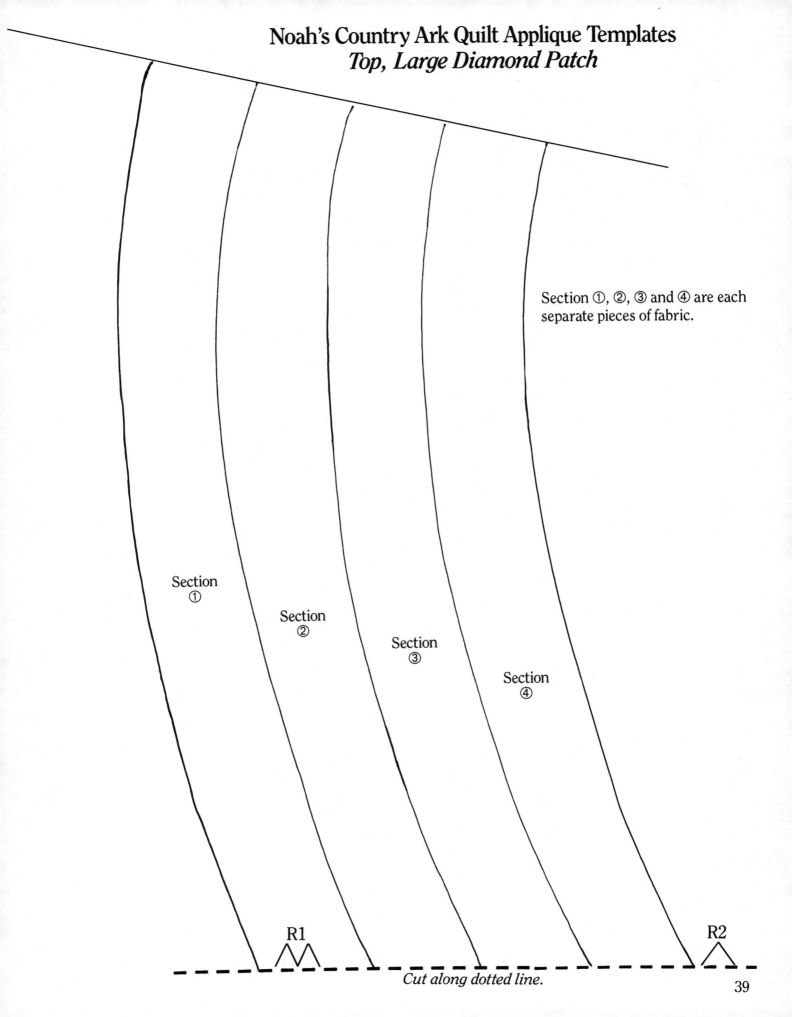

Section ①, ②, ③ and ④ are each separate pieces of fabric.

Section
①

Section
②

Section
③

Section
④

R1

R2

Cut along dotted line.

Noah's Country Ark Quilt Applique Layout
Left Side Triangle Patch

To create the finished layout, match corresponding letters/ numbers and notches along dotted lines and tape together. Complete Applique Layout will look like this:

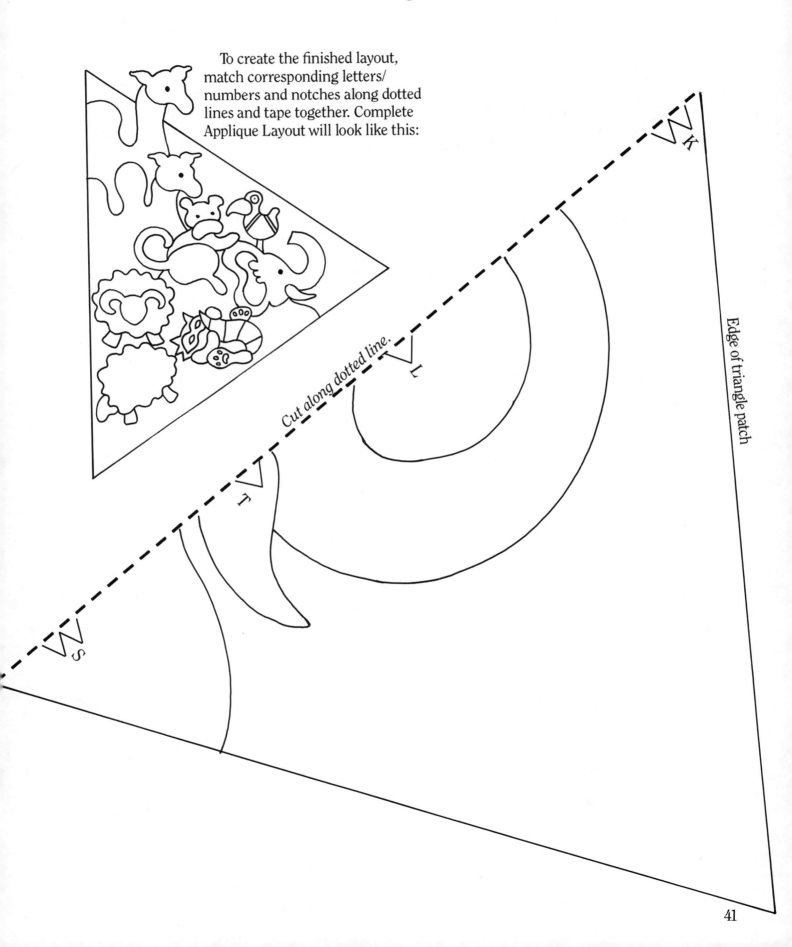

Cut along dotted line.

Edge of triangle patch

Cut along dotted line.

Noah's Country Ark Quilt Applique Layout
Left Side Triangle Patch

Note: Camel Head template overlaps onto Top, Large Diamond Patch.

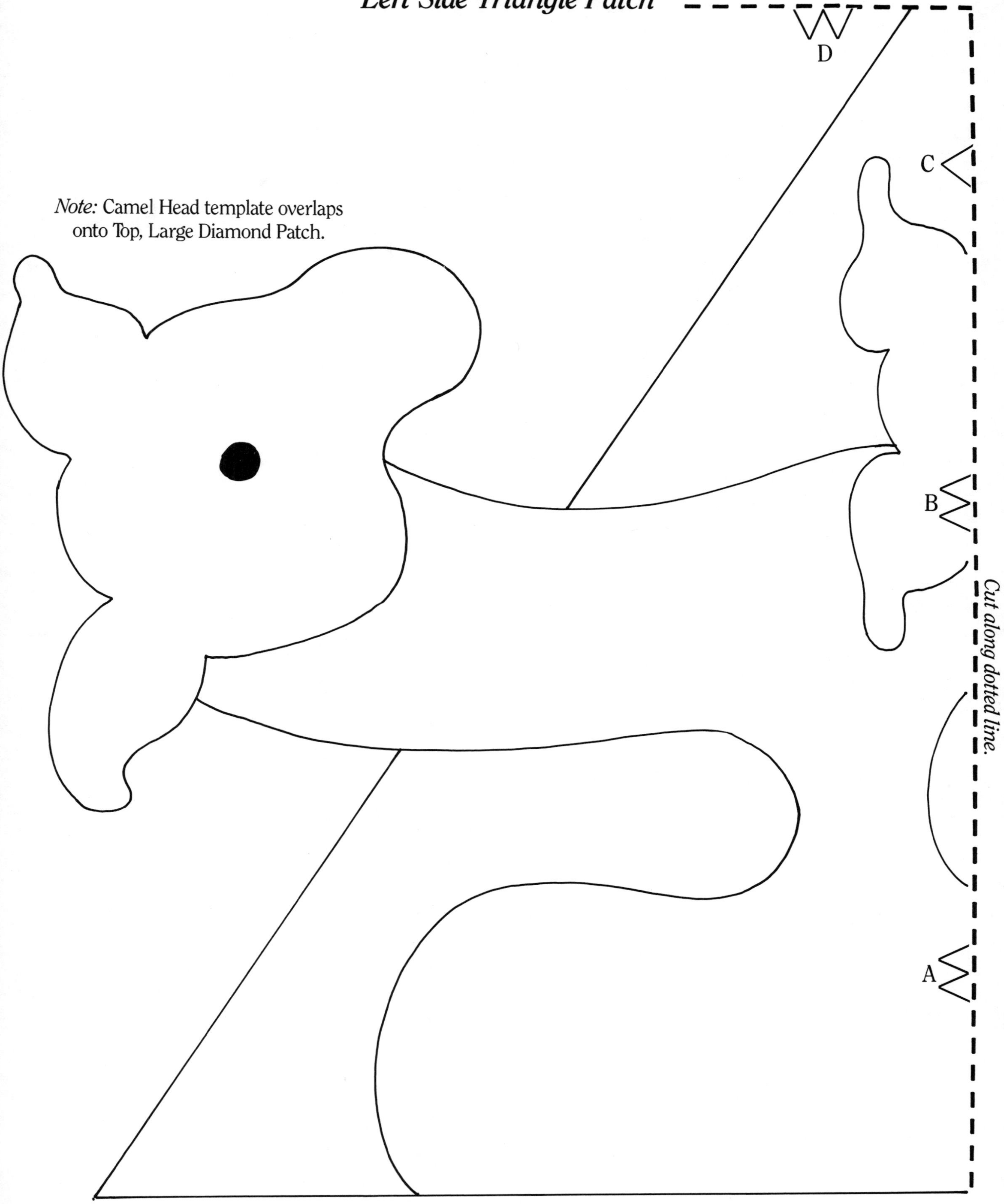
D
C
B
A
Cut along dotted line.

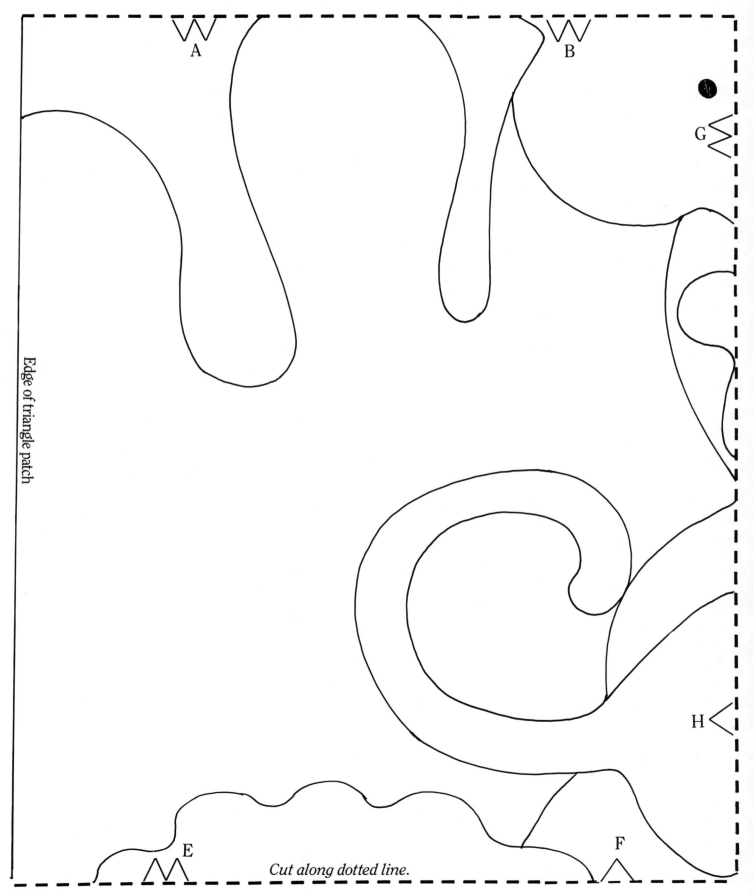

Edge of triangle patch

A

B

G

H

E

F

Cut along dotted line.

Noah's Country Ark Quilt Applique Layout
Left Side Triangle Patch

D

C

G

Cut along dotted line.

K

H

L

I

Q

J

Noah's Country Ark Quilt Applique Layout
Left Side Triangle Patch

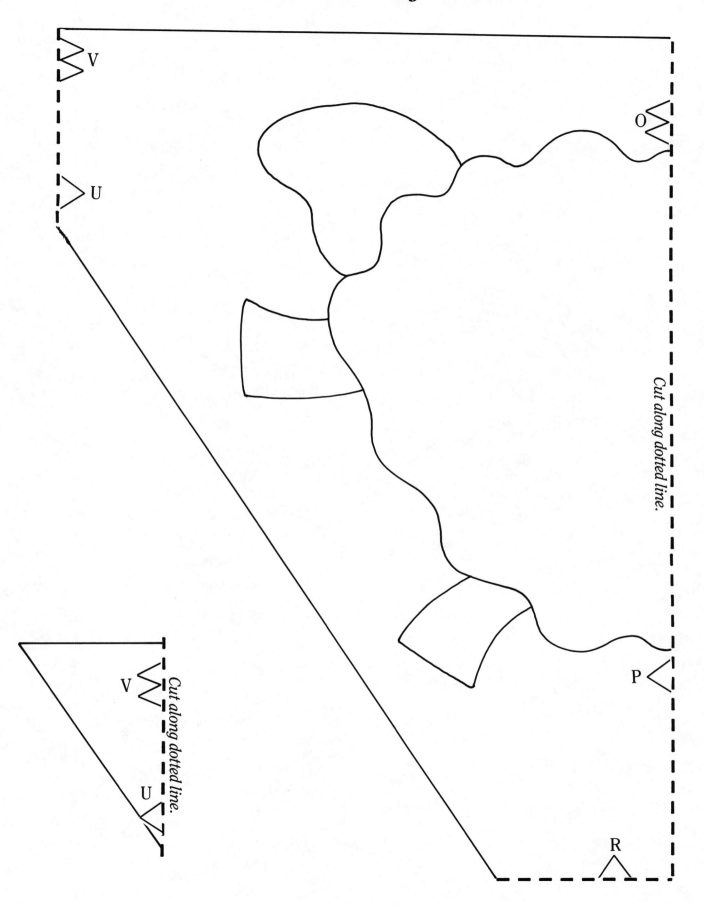

Cut along dotted line.

Cut along dotted line.

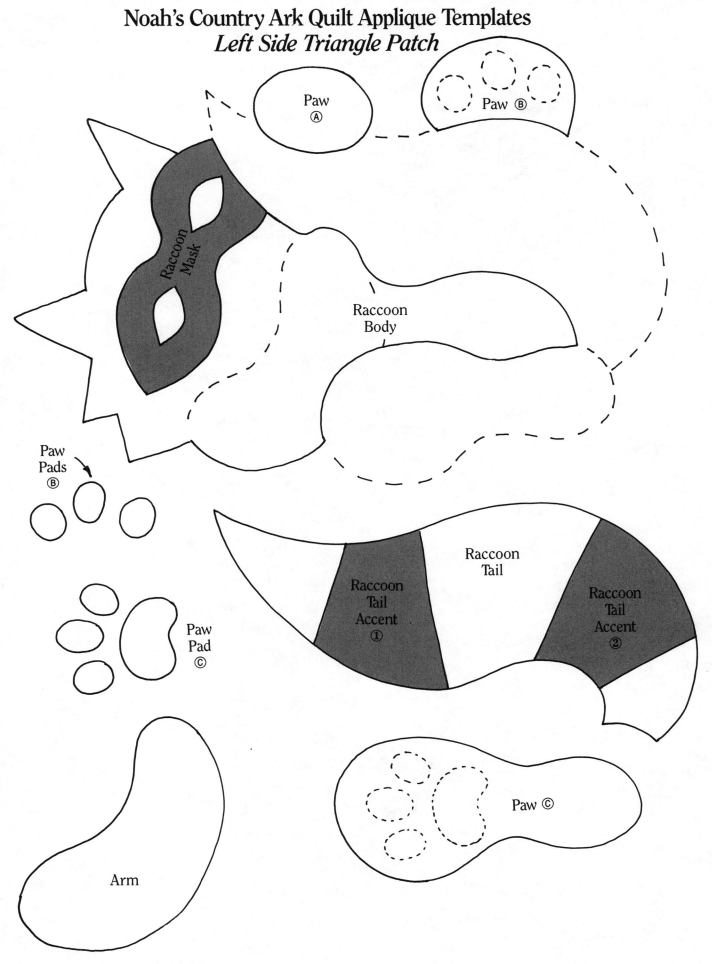

Paw Ⓐ

Paw Ⓑ

Raccoon Mask

Raccoon Body

Paw Pads Ⓑ

Paw Pad Ⓒ

Raccoon Tail Accent ①

Raccoon Tail

Raccoon Tail Accent ②

Arm

Paw Ⓒ

Noah's Country Ark Quilt Applique Templates
Left Side Triangle Patch

Sheep
Body

Sheep
Head

Sheep
Leg

Sheep
Leg

Bird
Beak

Bird
Eyeball

Tropical
Bird
Body

Tropical
Bird Body
Accent Stripes

Leg

Noah's Country Ark Quilt Applique Templates
Left Side Triangle Patch

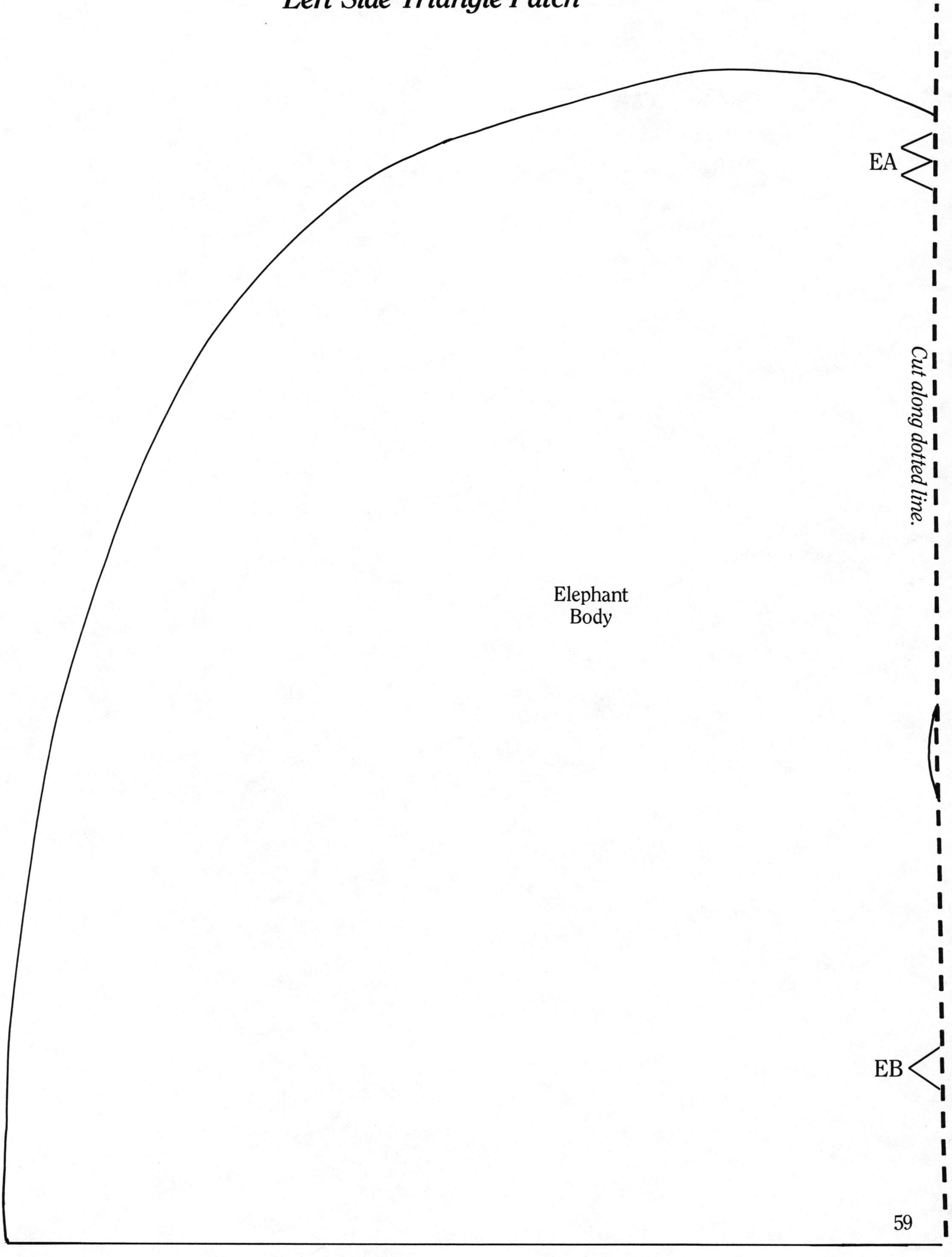
EA
Cut along dotted line.
Elephant Body
EB

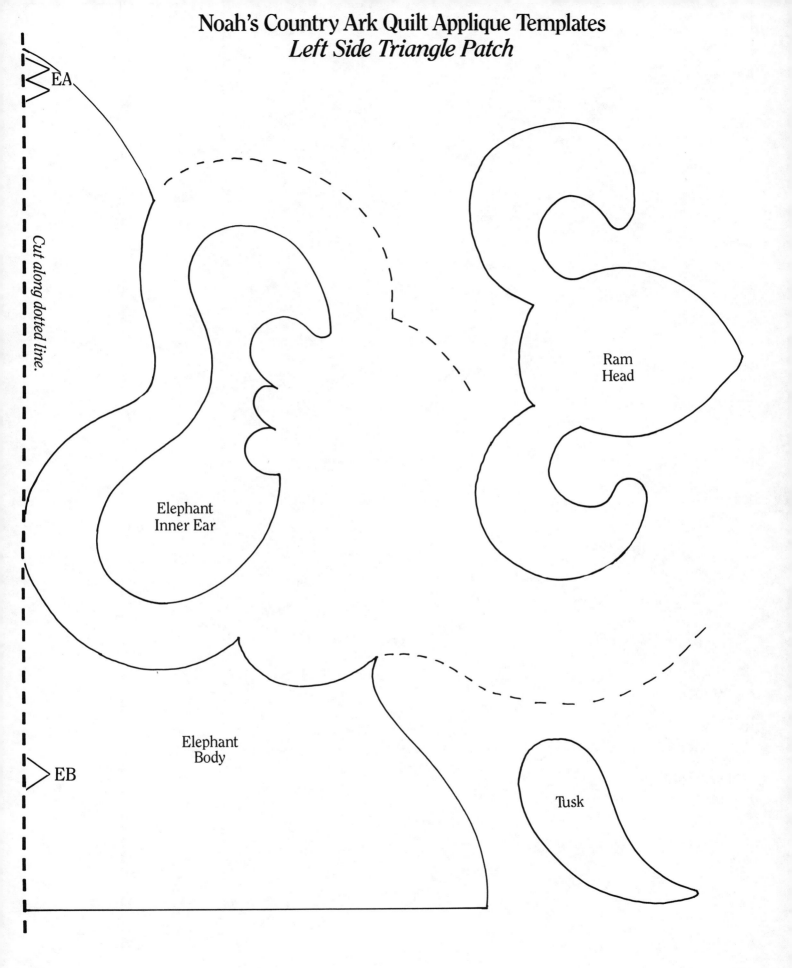

EA

Cut along dotted line.

Ram
Head

Elephant
Inner Ear

Elephant
Body

EB

Tusk

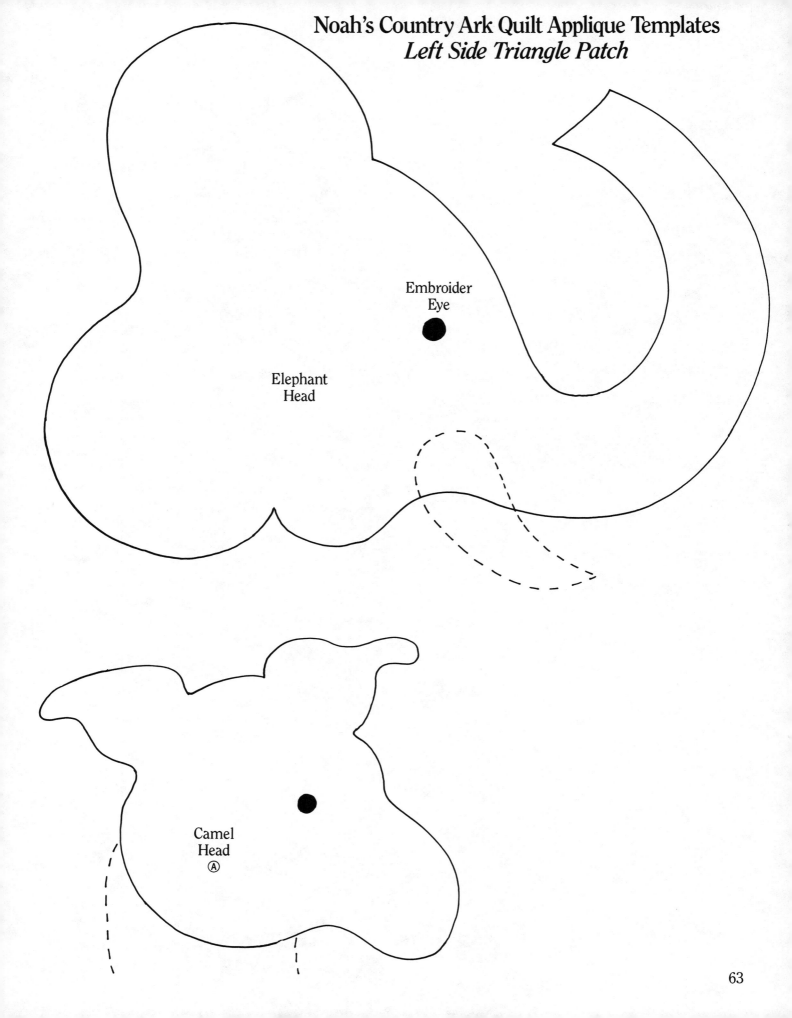

Embroider
Eye

Elephant
Head

Camel
Head
Ⓐ

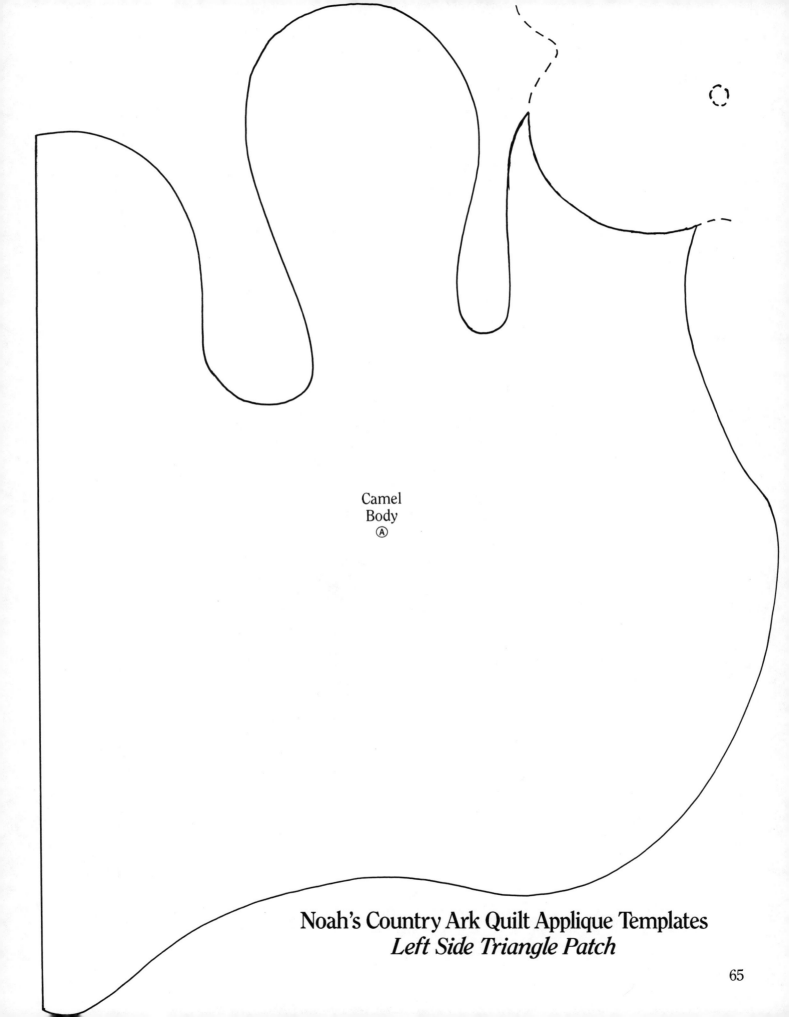

Camel
Body
Ⓐ

Noah's Country Ark Quilt Applique Templates
Left Side Triangle Patch

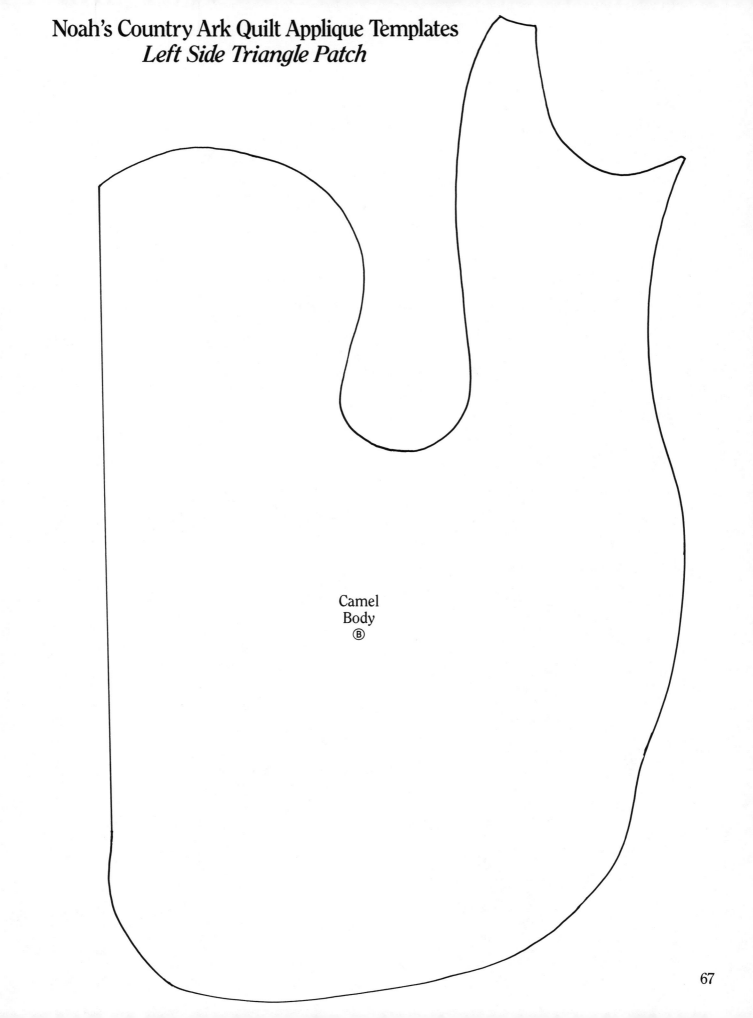

Camel
Body
Ⓑ

Noah's Country Ark Quilt Applique Templates
Left Side Triangle Patch

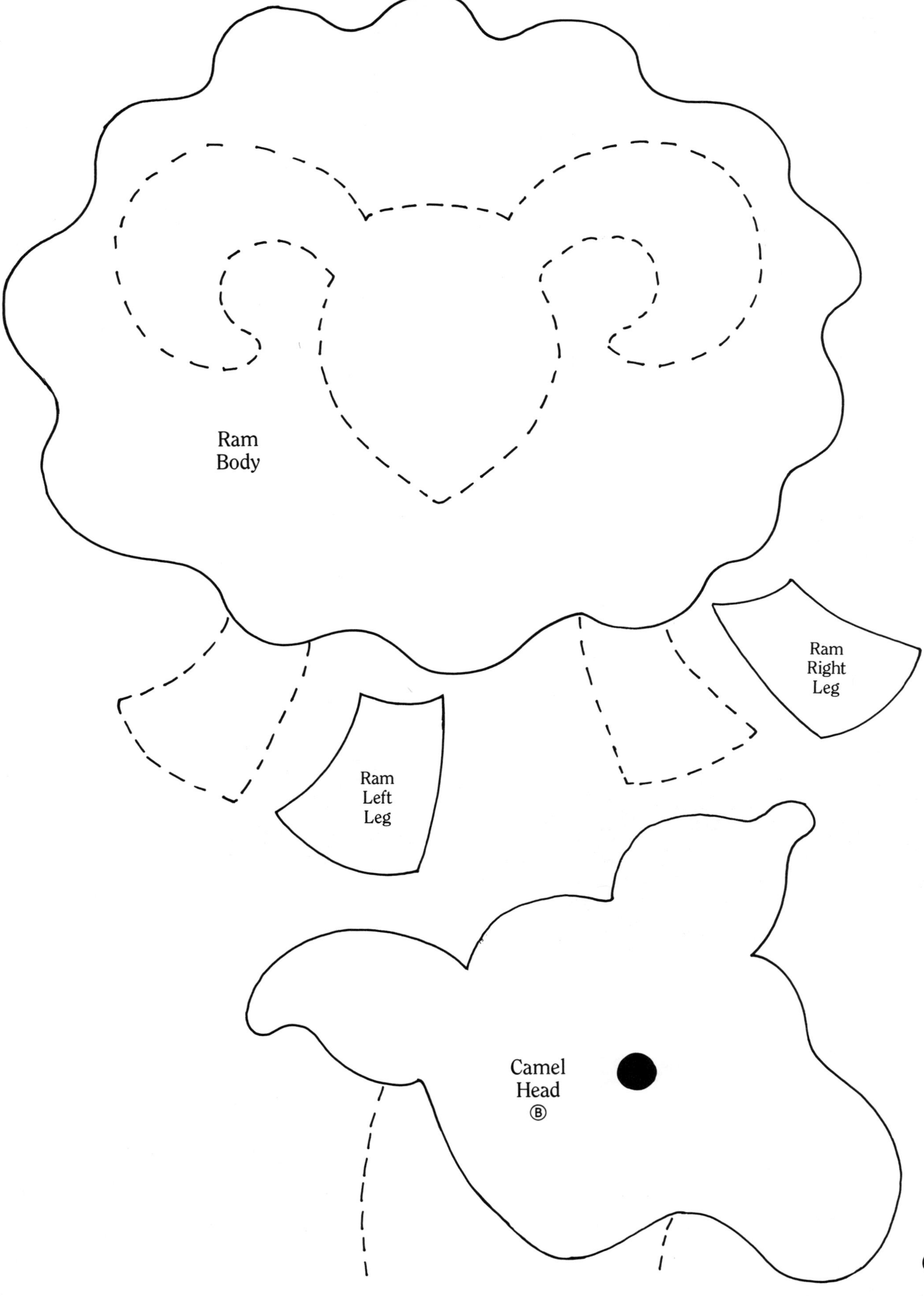
Ram Body
Ram Left Leg
Ram Right Leg
Camel Head
Ⓑ

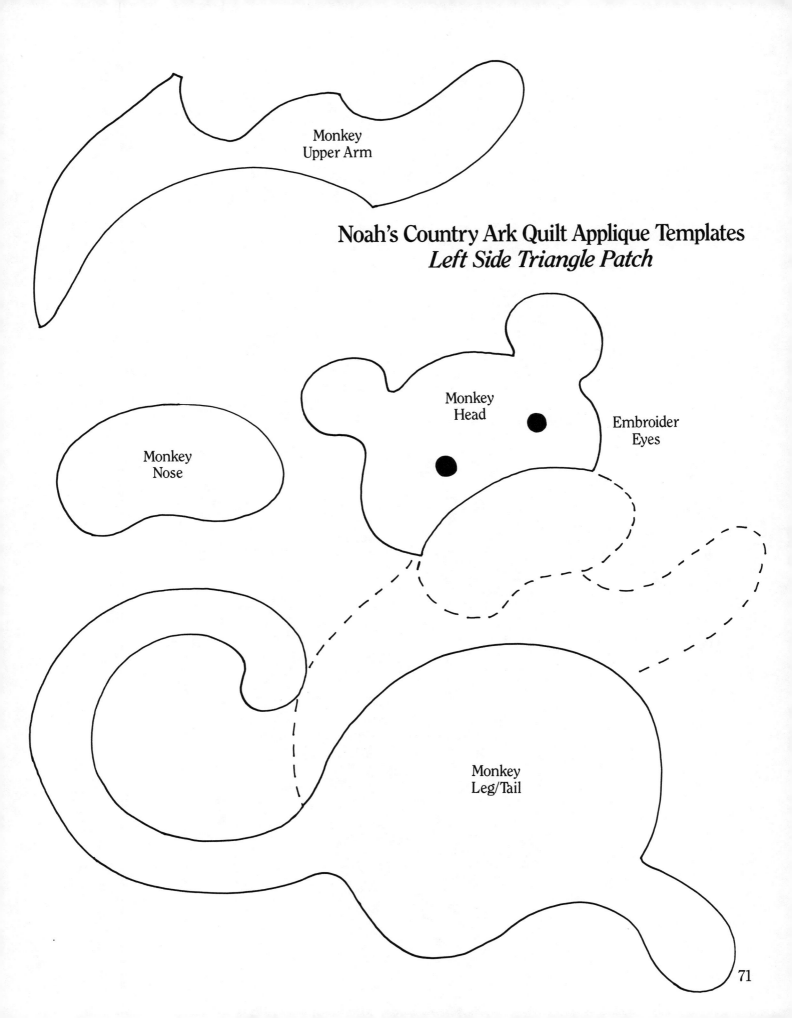

Monkey
Upper Arm

Noah's Country Ark Quilt Applique Templates
Left Side Triangle Patch

Monkey
Head

Embroider
Eyes

Monkey
Nose

Monkey
Leg/Tail

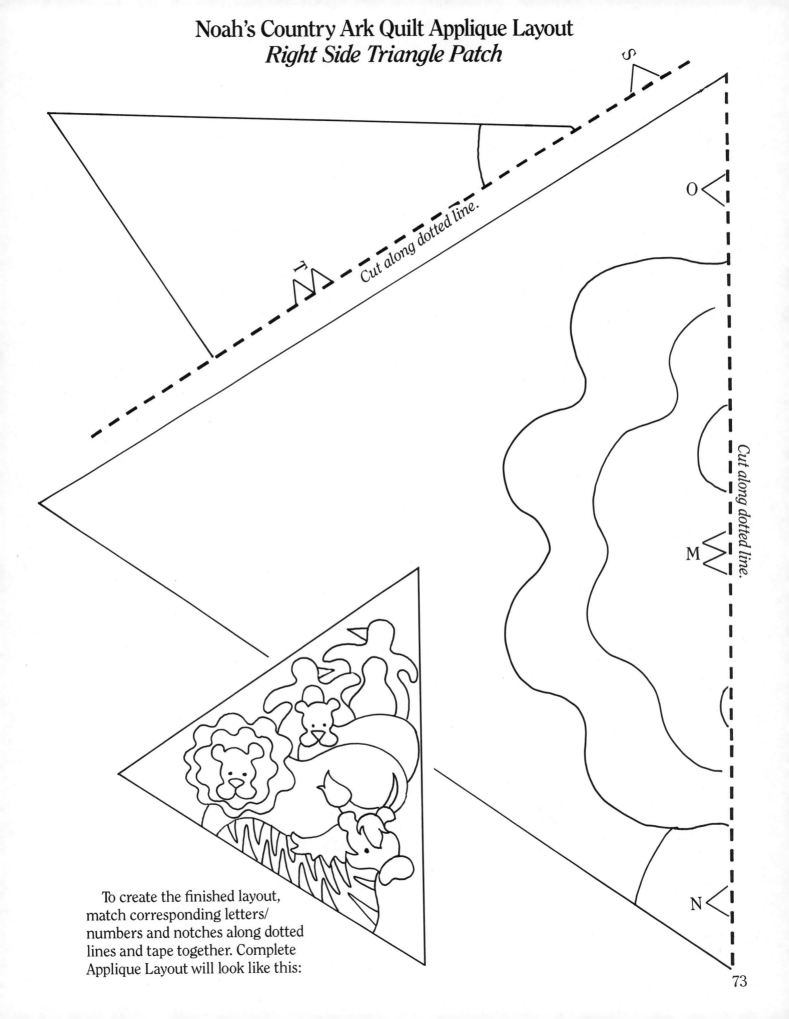

Cut along dotted line.

Cut along dotted line.

To create the finished layout, match corresponding letters/ numbers and notches along dotted lines and tape together. Complete Applique Layout will look like this:

Noah's Country Ark Quilt Applique Layout
Right Side Triangle Patch

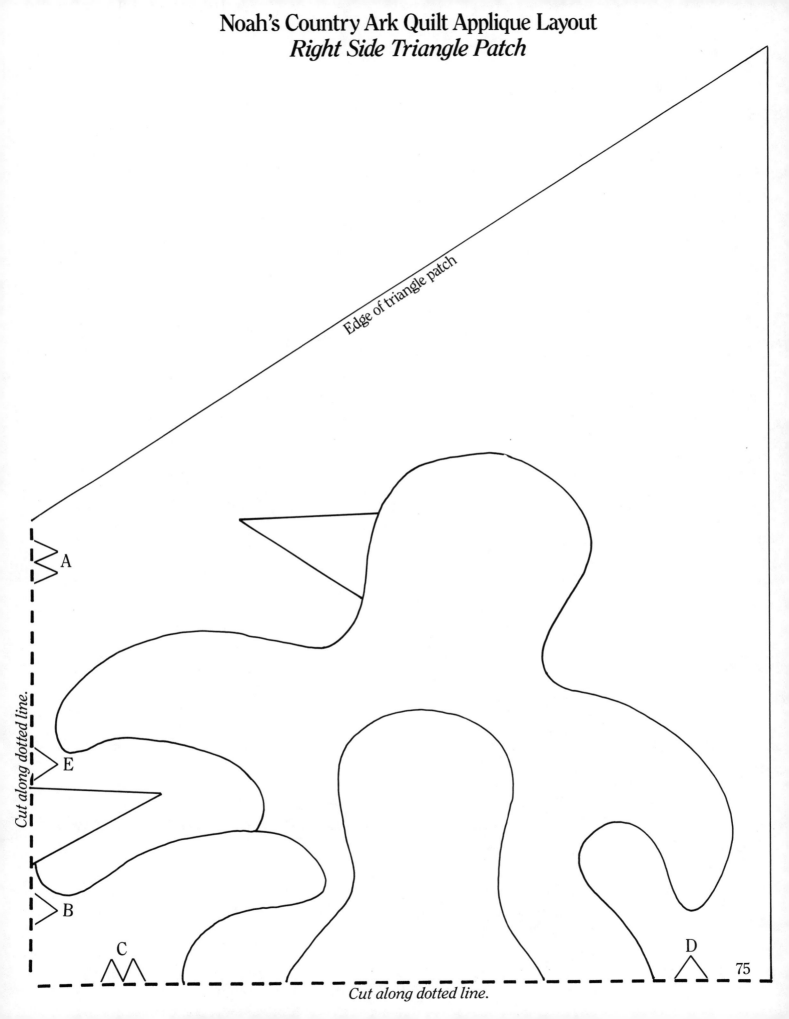

Edge of triangle patch

Cut along dotted line.

A

E

B

C

D

75

Cut along dotted line.

Noah's Country Ark Quilt Applique Layout
Right Side Triangle Patch
Cut along dotted line.

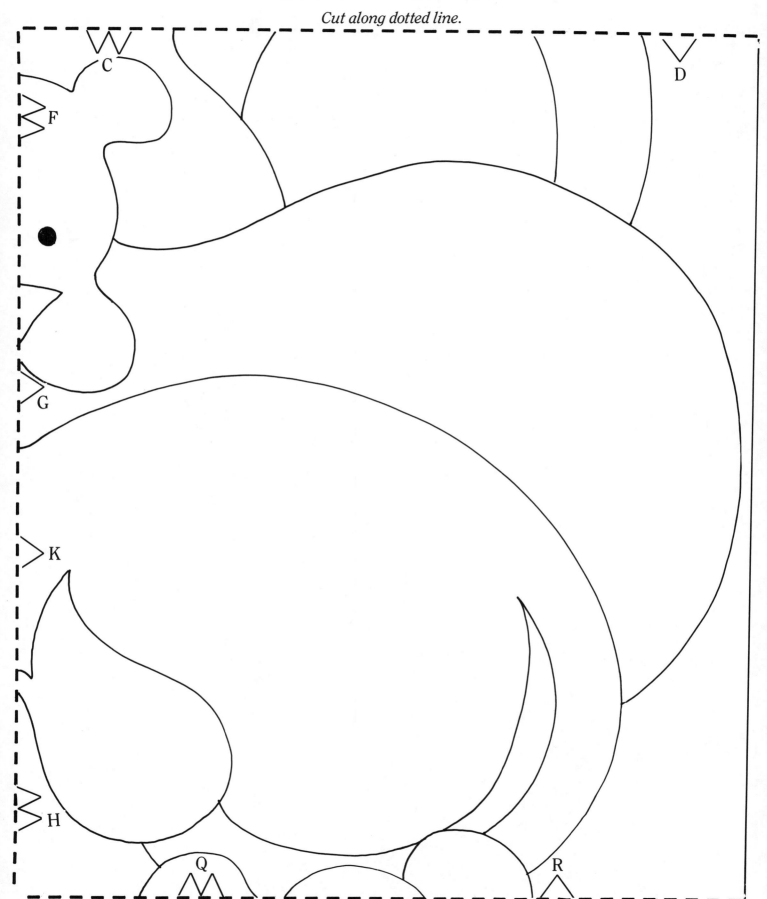

C

F

D

G

K

H

Q

R

Cut along dotted line.

Noah's Country Ark Quilt Applique Layout
Right Side Triangle Patch

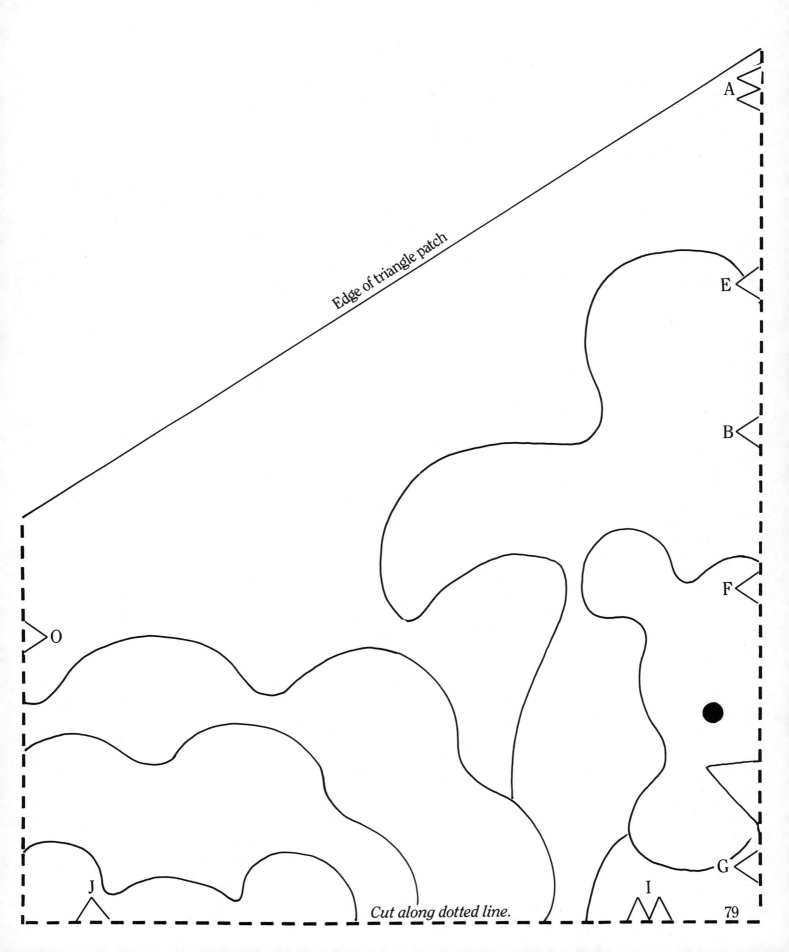

Edge of triangle patch

A

E

B

F

O

G

J

I

Cut along dotted line.

Noah's Country Ark Quilt Applique Layout
Right Side Triangle Patch

Cut along dotted line.

Cut along dotted line.

Cut along dotted line.

Cut along dotted line.

R

T

Q

S

P

L

O

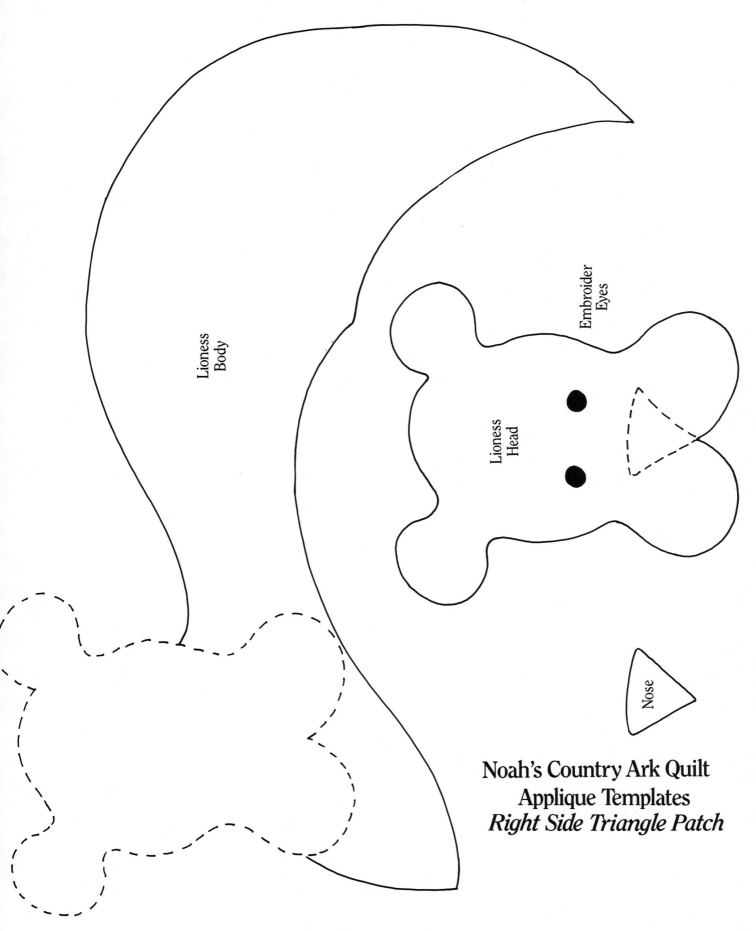

Lioness
Body

Embroider
Eyes

Lioness
Head

Nose

Noah's Country Ark Quilt
Applique Templates
Right Side Triangle Patch

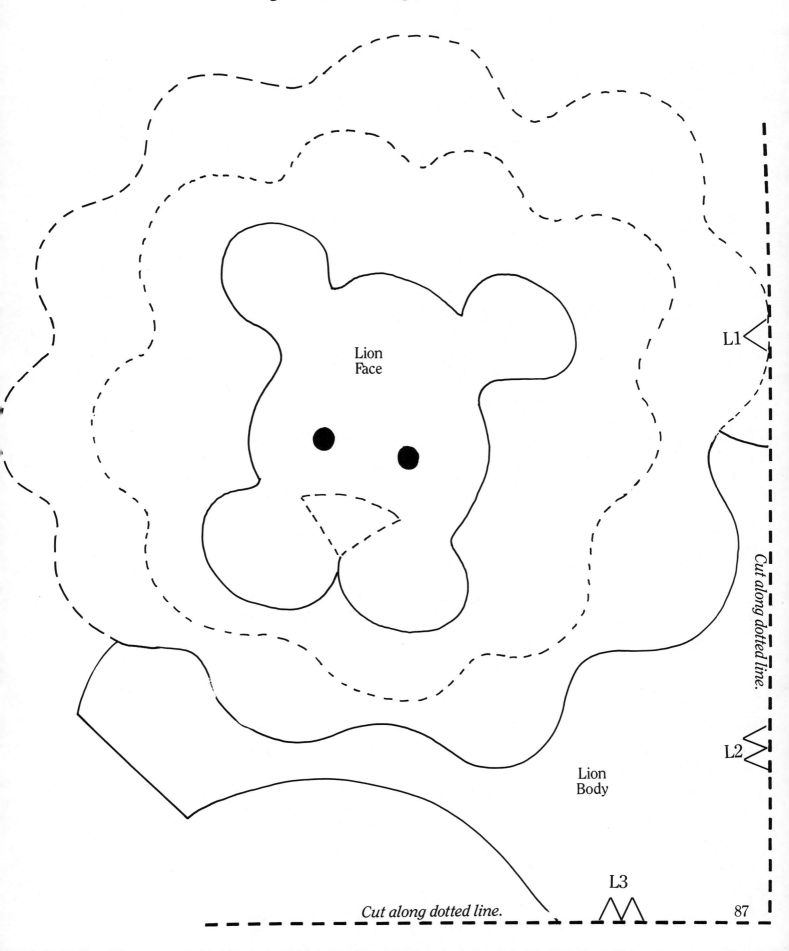

Lion
Face

Lion
Body

L1

L2

L3

Cut along dotted line.

Cut along dotted line.

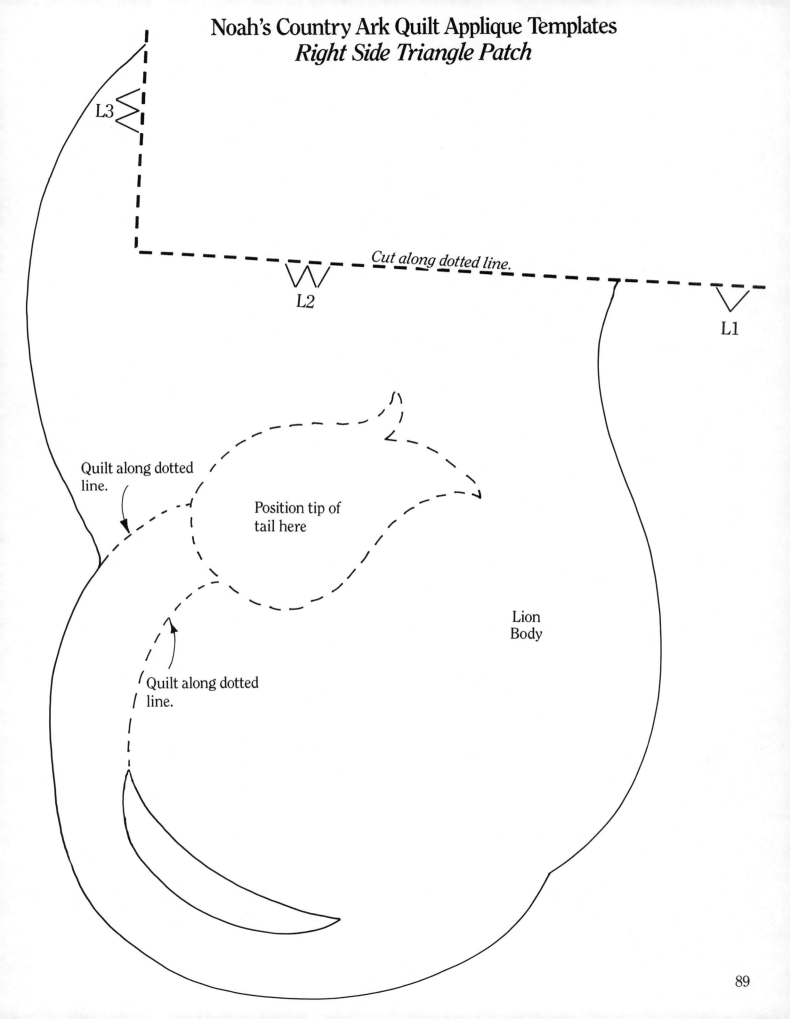

L3

L2

L1

Cut along dotted line.

Quilt along dotted line.

Position tip of tail here

Lion Body

Quilt along dotted line.

Noah's Country Ark Quilt Applique Templates
Right Side Triangle Patch

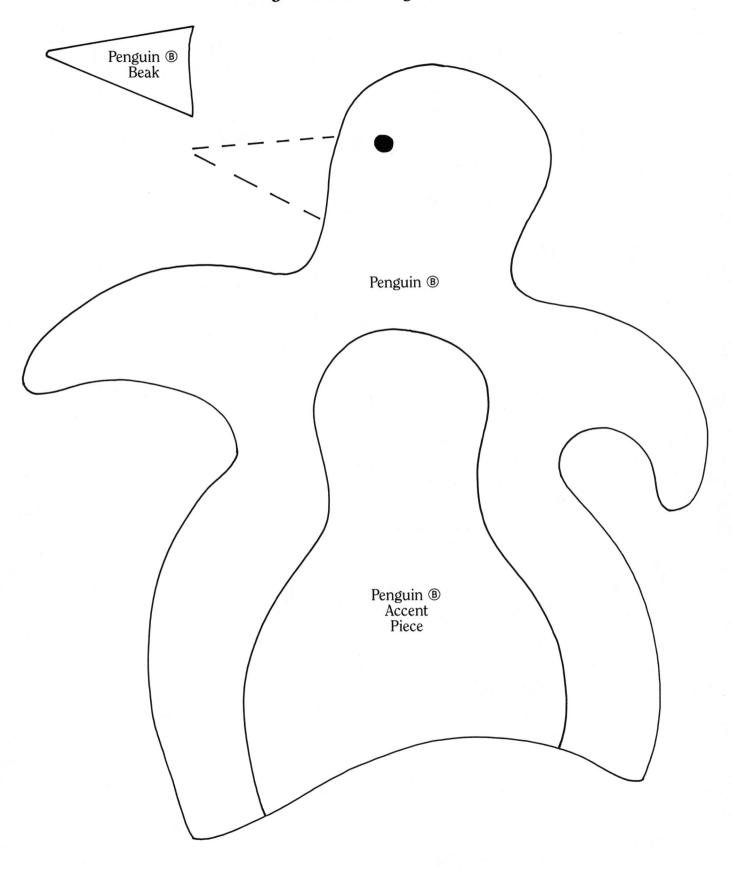

Penguin Ⓑ
Beak

Penguin Ⓑ

Penguin Ⓑ
Accent
Piece

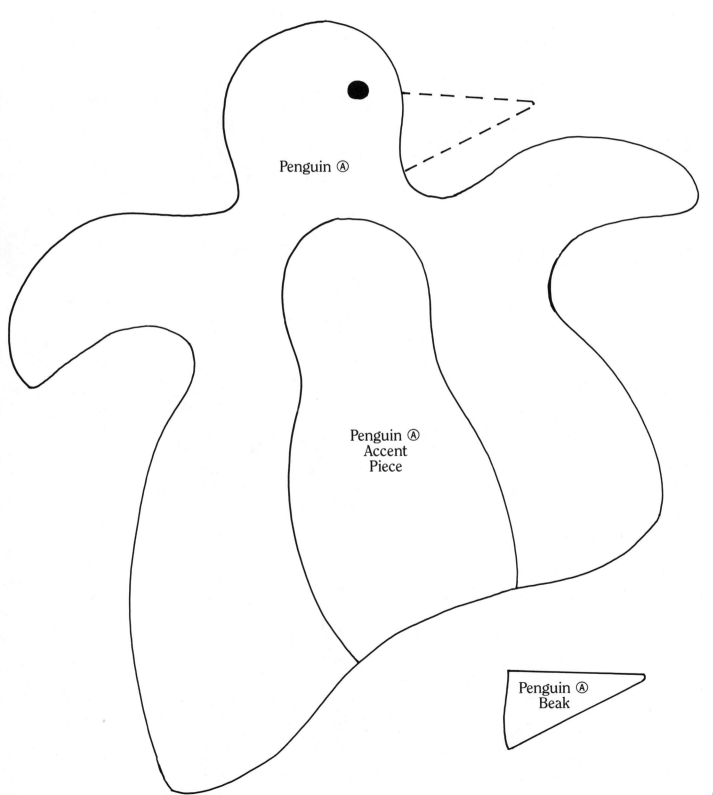

Penguin Ⓐ

Penguin Ⓐ
Accent
Piece

Penguin Ⓐ
Beak

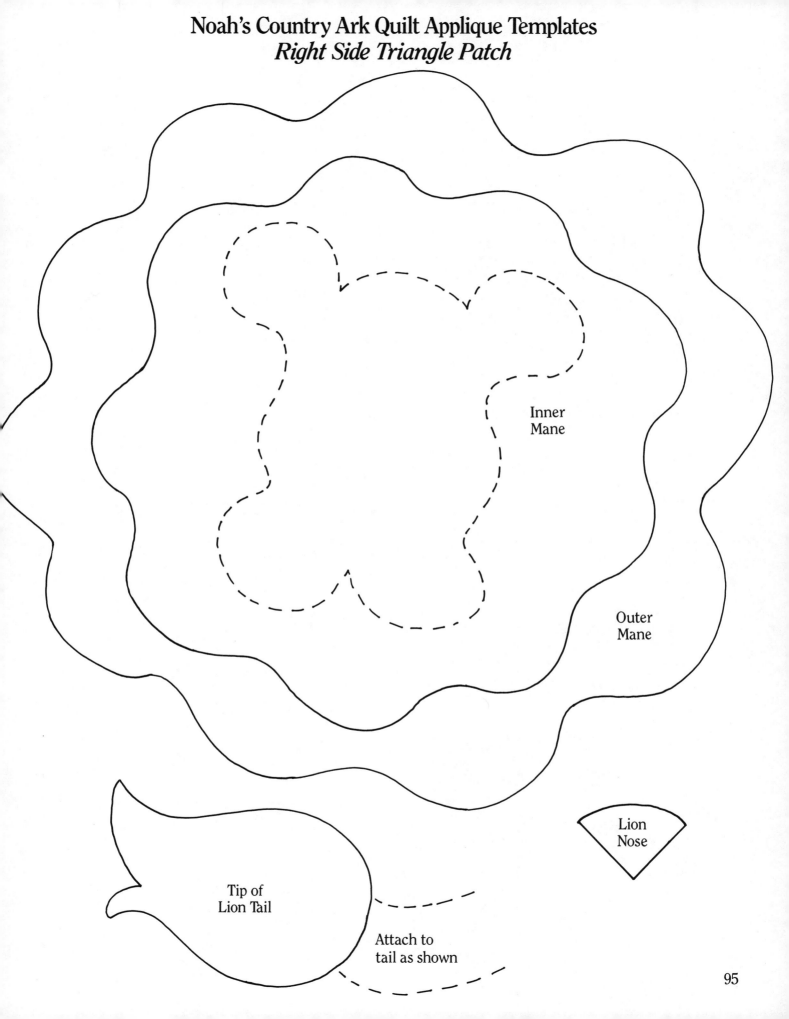

Inner Mane

Outer Mane

Lion Nose

Tip of Lion Tail

Attach to tail as shown

95

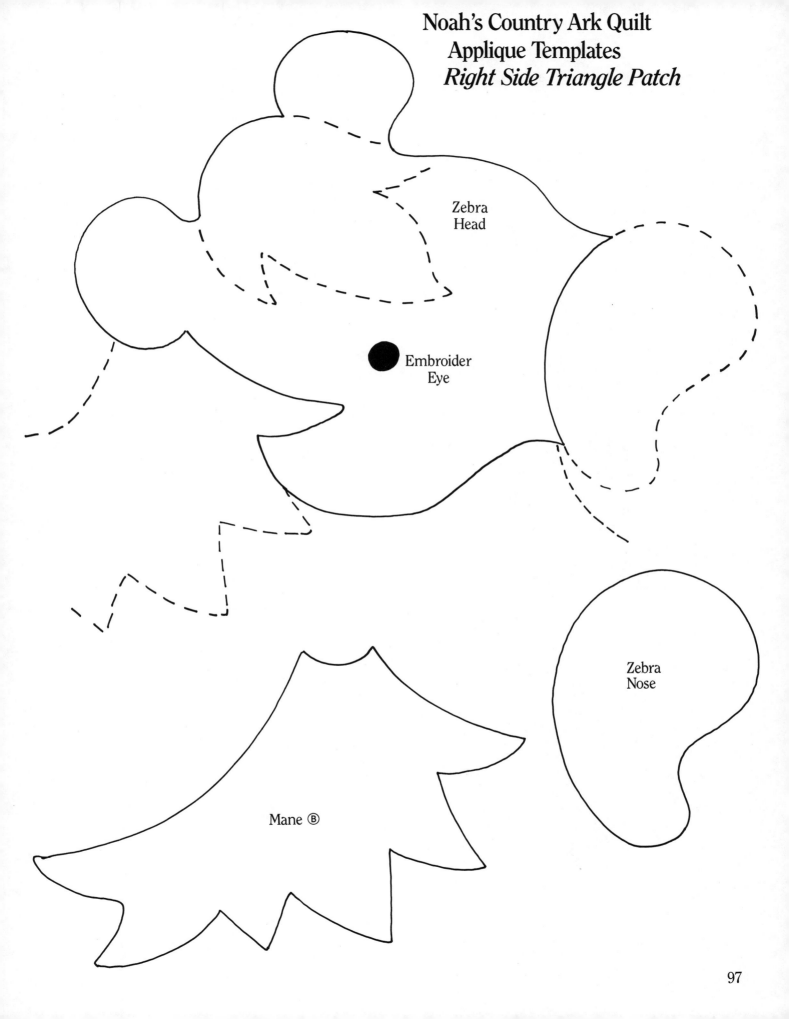

Zebra
Head

Embroider
Eye

Zebra
Nose

Mane ®

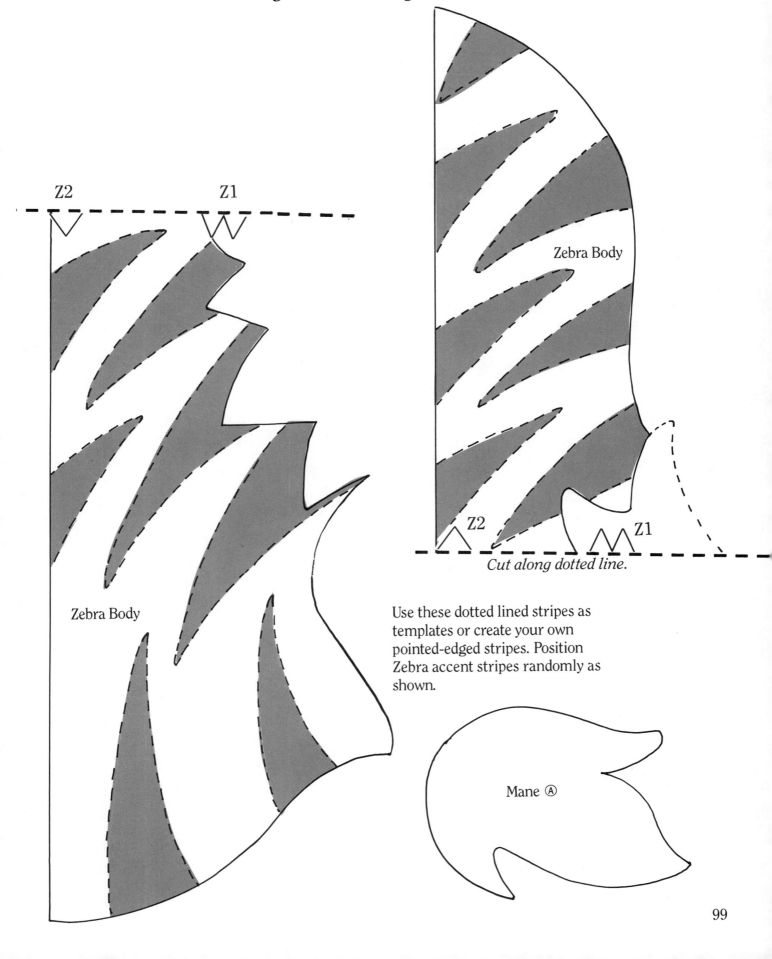

Z2 Z1

Zebra Body

Zebra Body

Z2 Z1

Cut along dotted line.

Use these dotted lined stripes as templates or create your own pointed-edged stripes. Position Zebra accent stripes randomly as shown.

Mane Ⓐ

Noah's Country Ark Quilt Applique Layout
Large, Bottom Diamond Patch

To create the finished layout, match corresponding letters/ numbers and notches along dotted lines and tape together. Complete Applique Layout will look like this:

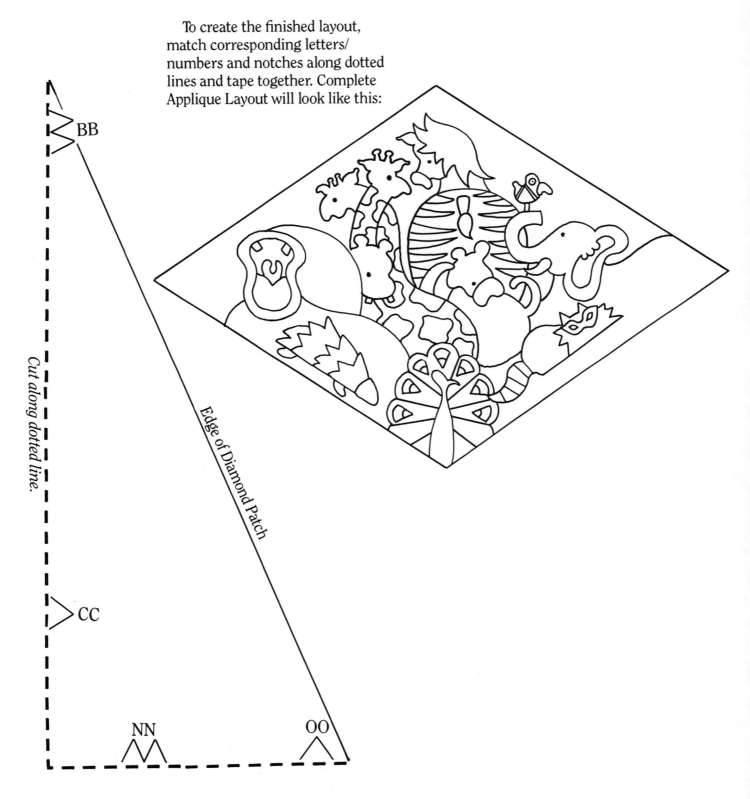

BB

Cut along dotted line.

Edge of Diamond Patch

CC

NN

OO

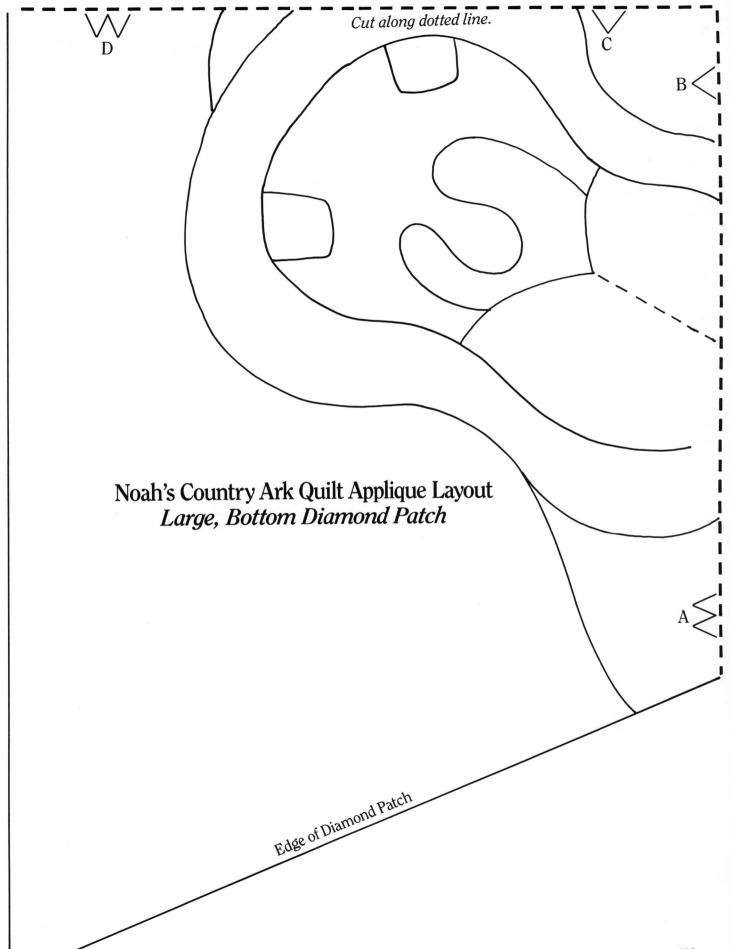

Cut along dotted line.

D

C

B

A

Noah's Country Ark Quilt Applique Layout
Large, Bottom Diamond Patch

Edge of Diamond Patch

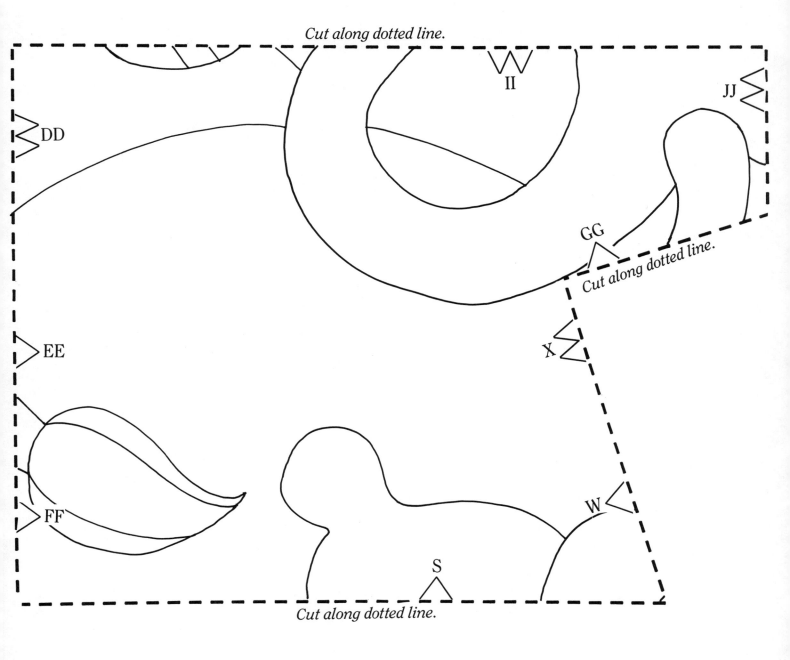

Cut along dotted line.

Cut along dotted line.

Cut along dotted line.

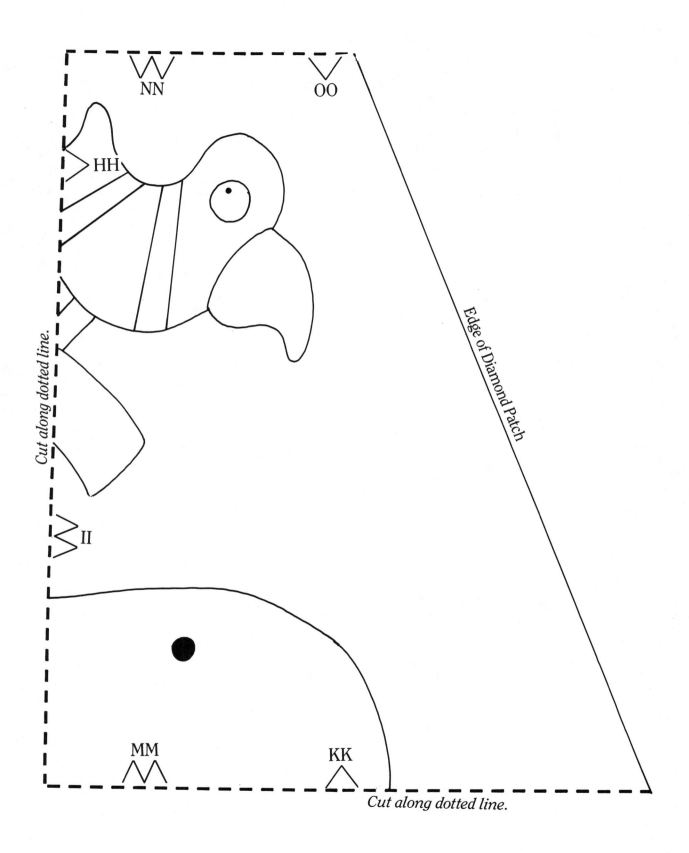

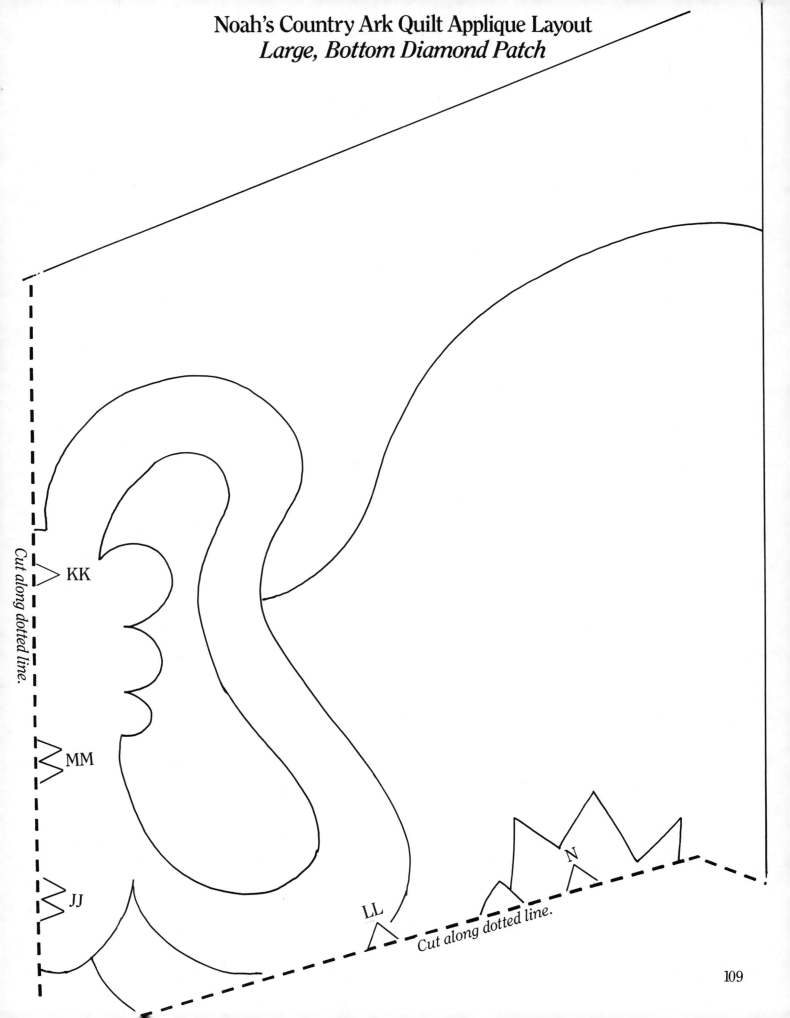

Cut along dotted line.

KK

MM

JJ

LL

N

Cut along dotted line.

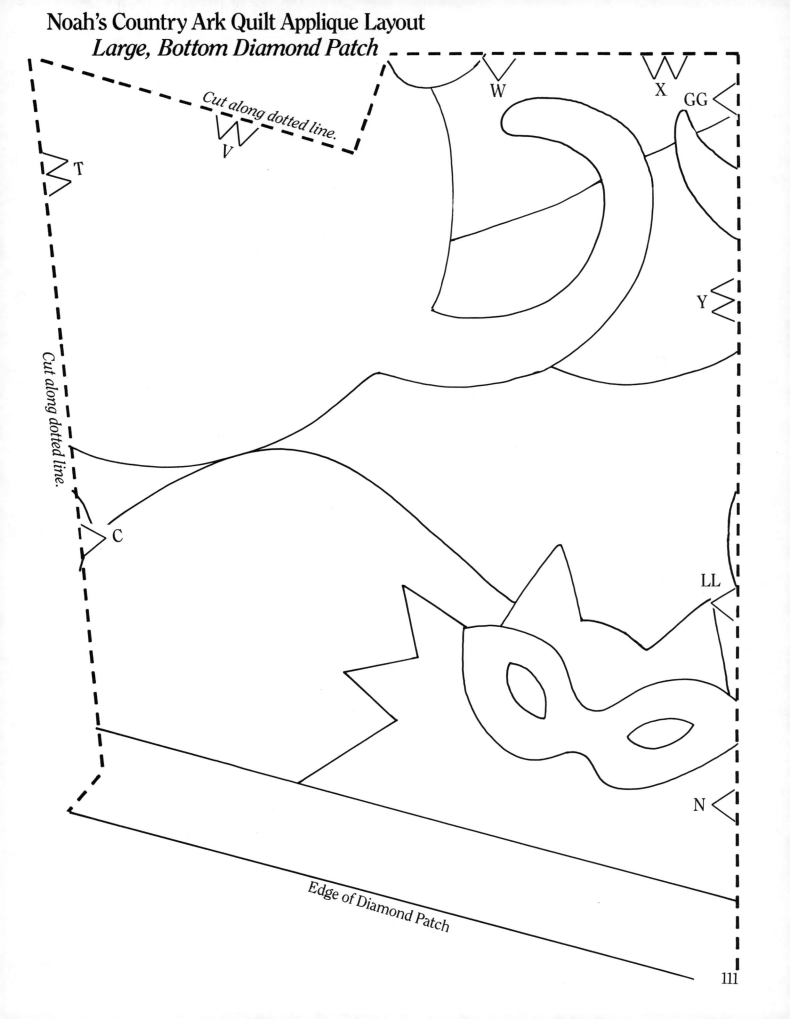

Noah's Country Ark Quilt Applique Layout
Large, Bottom Diamond Patch

Cut along dotted line.

Cut along dotted line.

W

V

X

GG

T

Y

C

LL

N

Edge of Diamond Patch

111

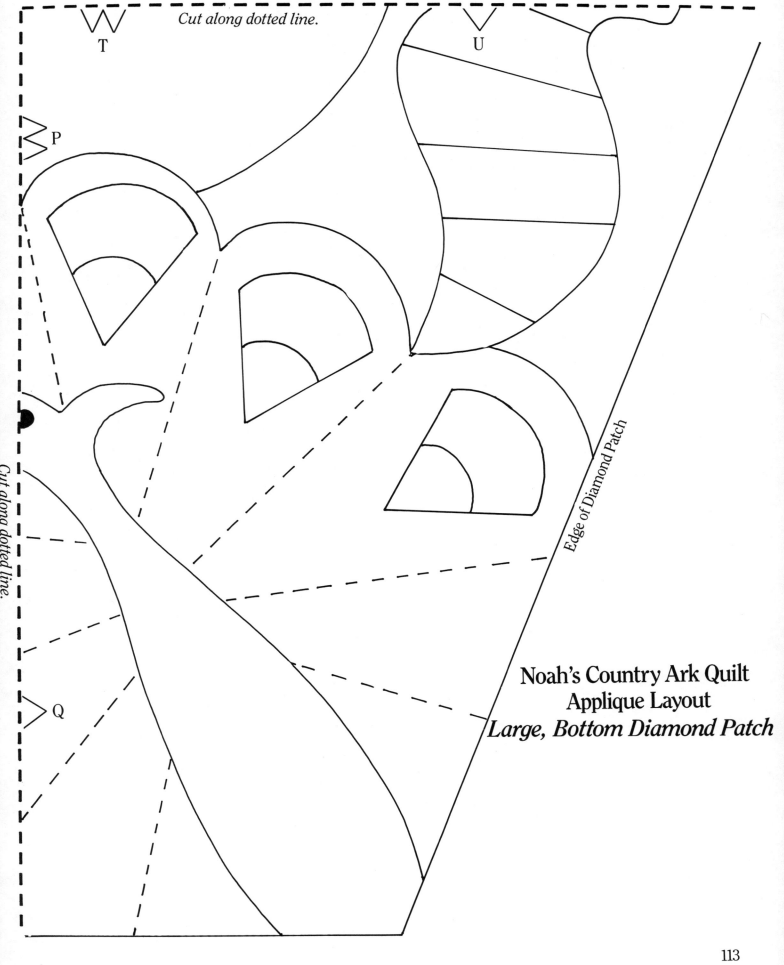

Cut along dotted line.

T

P

U

Cut along dotted line.

Edge of Diamond Patch

Q

Noah's Country Ark Quilt
Applique Layout
Large, Bottom Diamond Patch

113

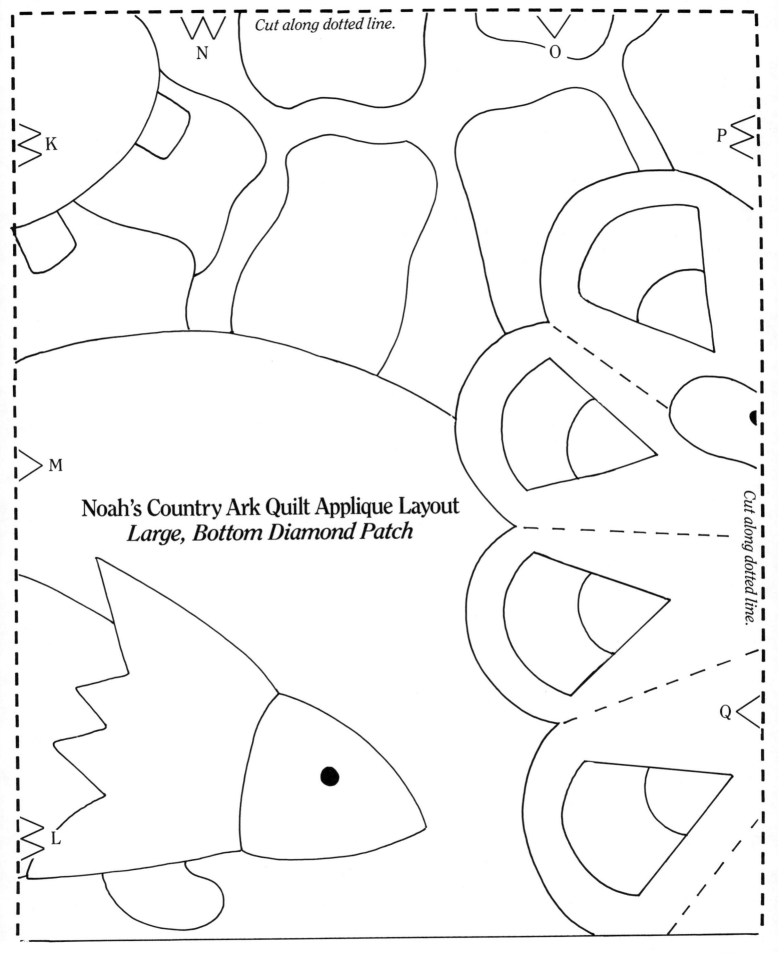

Cut along dotted line.

Noah's Country Ark Quilt Applique Layout
Large, Bottom Diamond Patch

Cut along dotted line.

Noah's Country Ark Quilt Applique Layout
Large, Bottom Diamond Patch

Cut along dotted line.

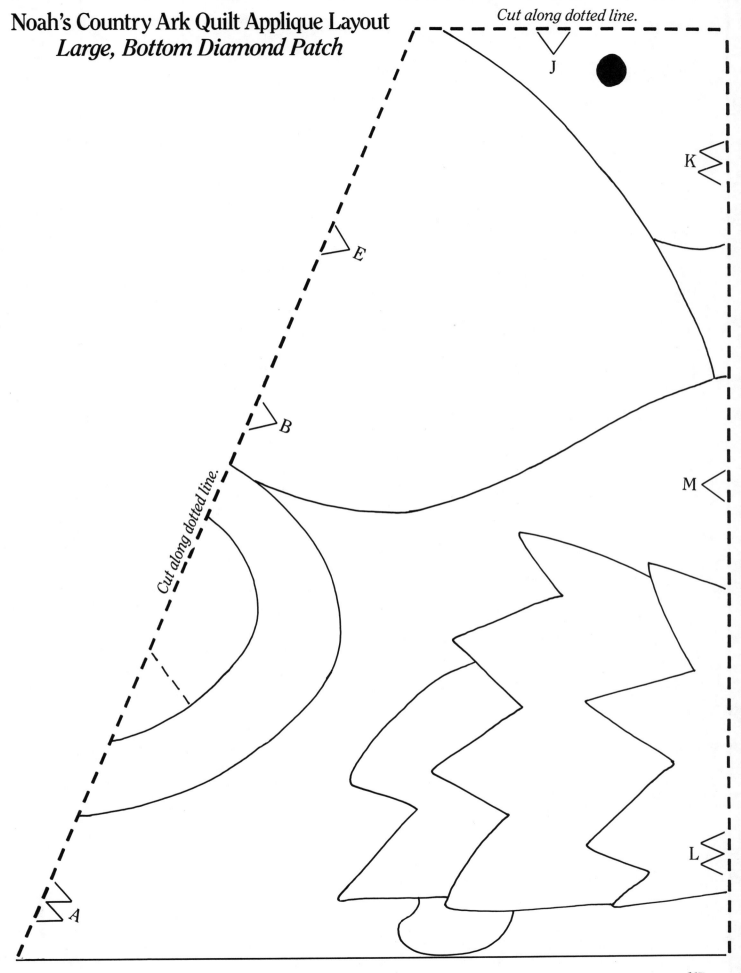

Cut along dotted line.

J

K

E

B

M

A

L

117

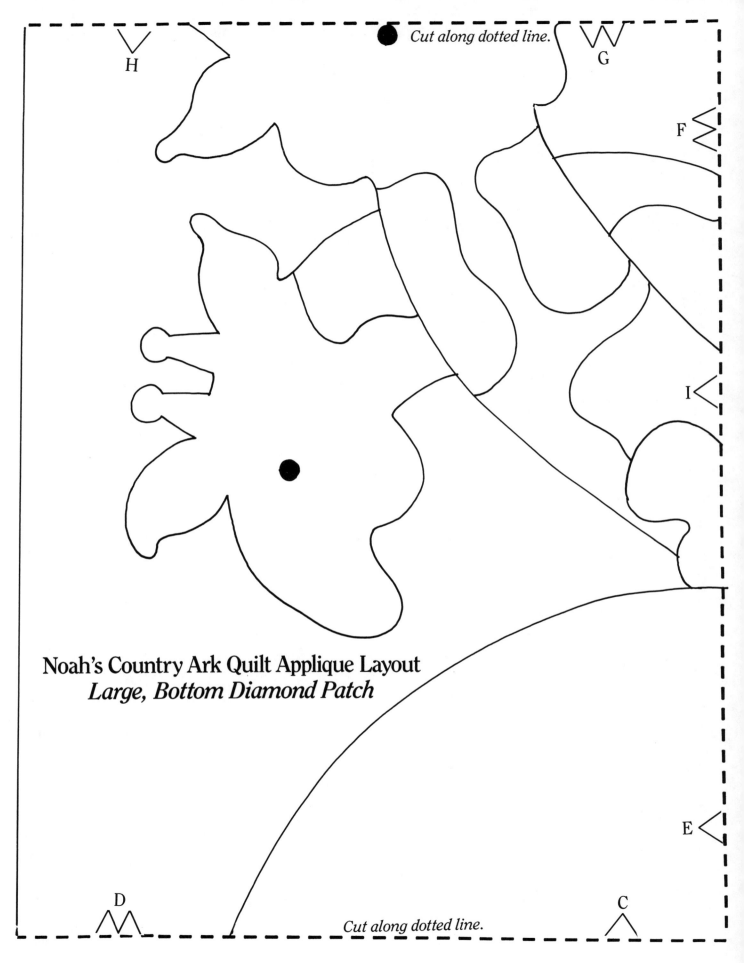

H

G

F

Cut along dotted line.

I

Noah's Country Ark Quilt Applique Layout
Large, Bottom Diamond Patch

E

D

C

Cut along dotted line.

119

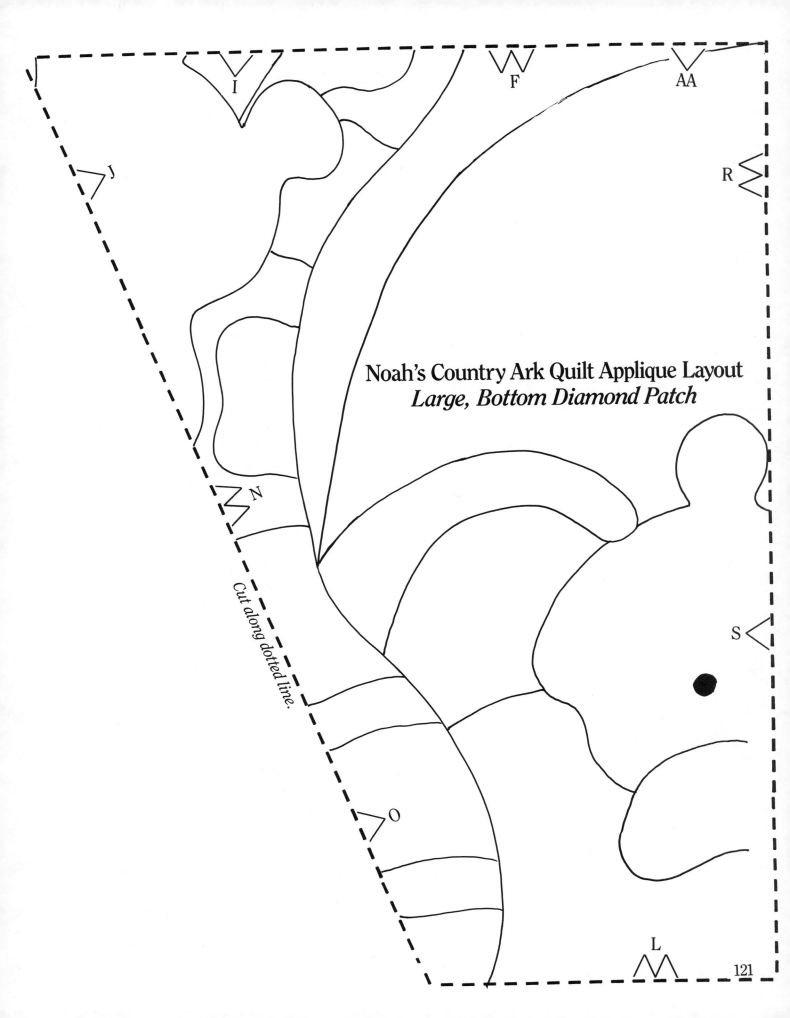

I

J

W
F

AA

R

Noah's Country Ark Quilt Applique Layout
Large, Bottom Diamond Patch

N

S

Cut along dotted line.

O

L

121

Noah's Country Ark Quilt Applique Layout
Large, Bottom Diamond Patch

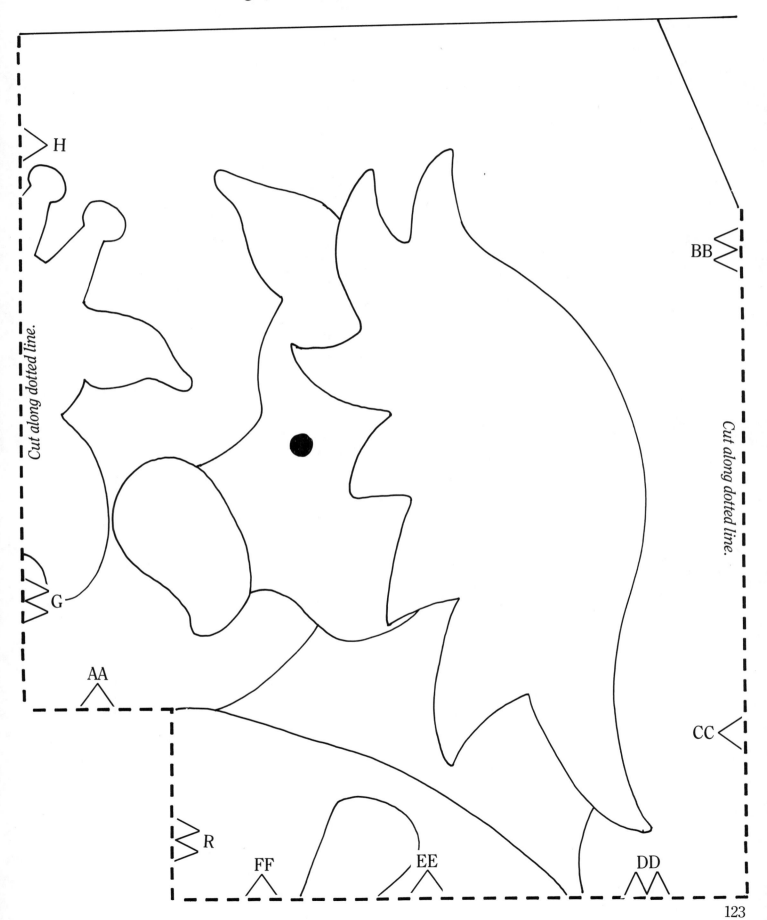

Cut along dotted line.

Cut along dotted line.

H

BB

G

AA

R

FF

EE

DD

CC

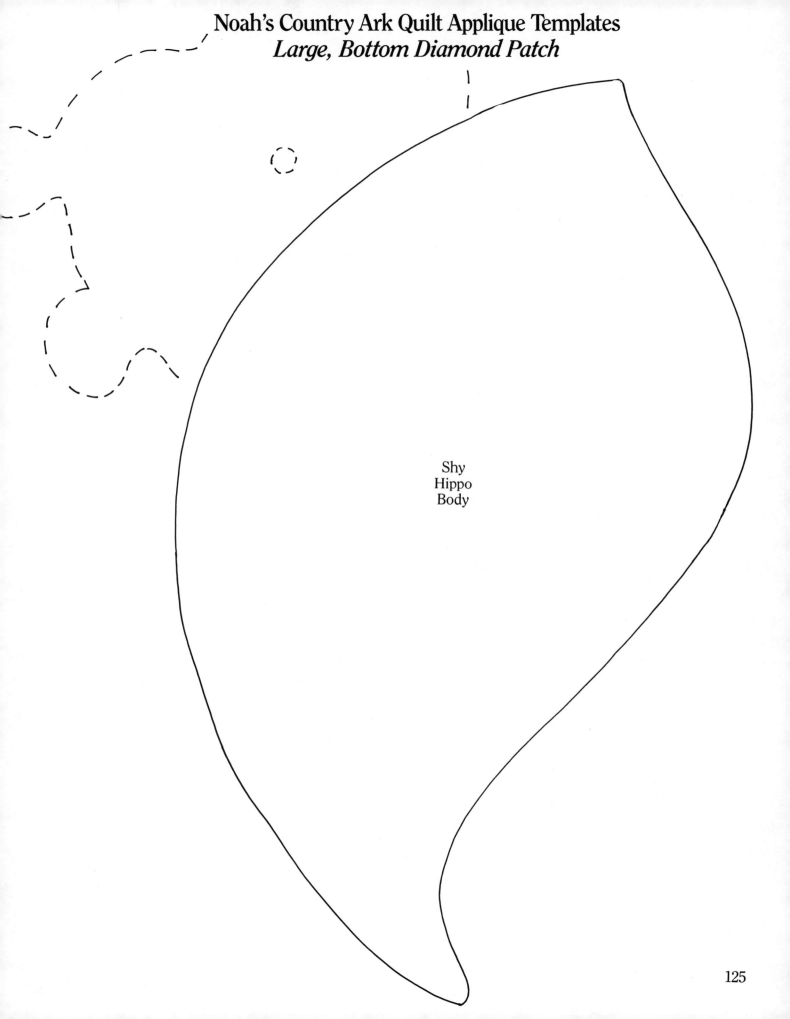

Shy
Hippo
Body

Noah's Country Ark Quilt Applique Templates
Large, Bottom Diamond Patch

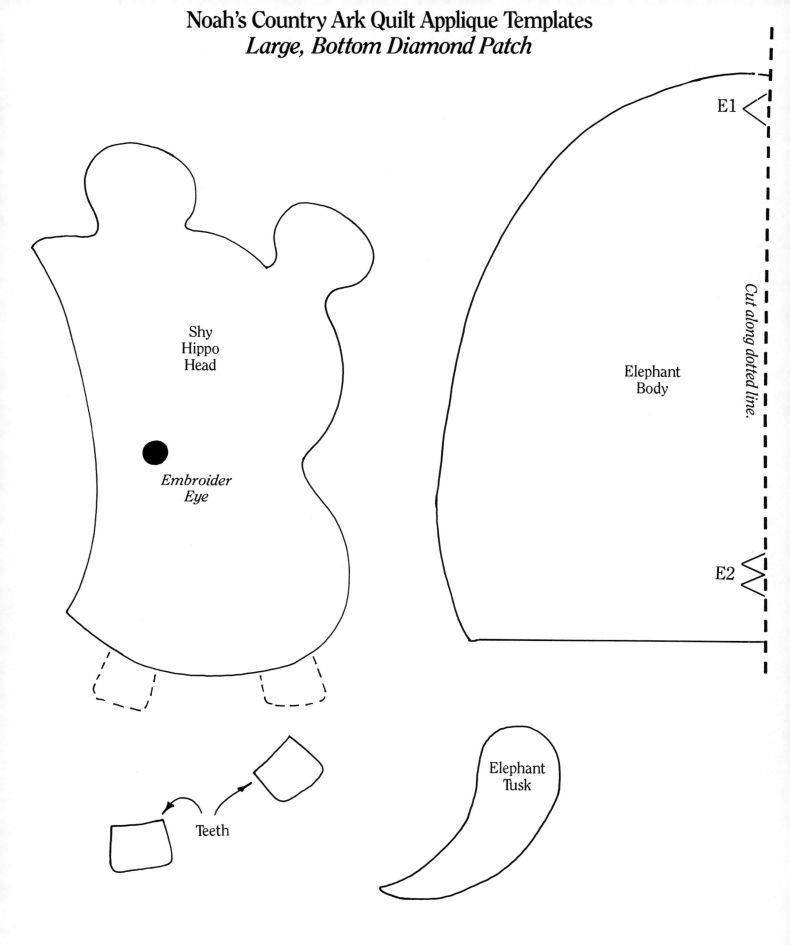

E1

Elephant
Body

Cut along dotted line.

E2

Shy
Hippo
Head

*Embroider
Eye*

Teeth

Elephant
Tusk

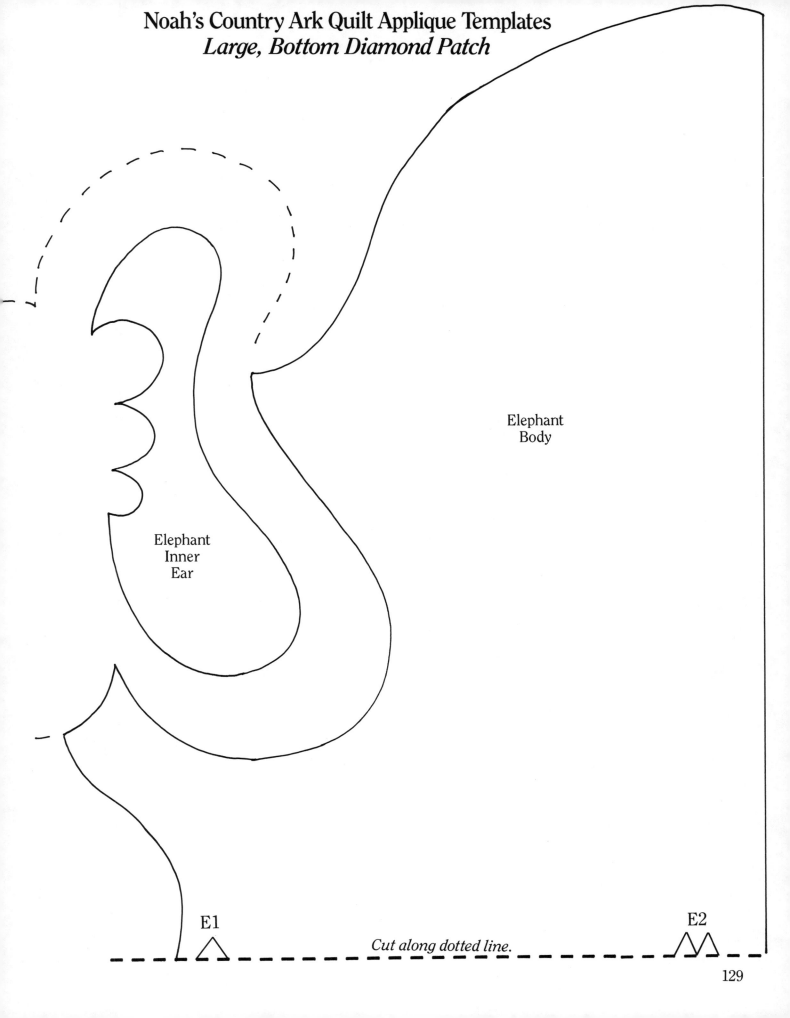

Elephant
Body

Elephant
Inner
Ear

E1

E2

Cut along dotted line.

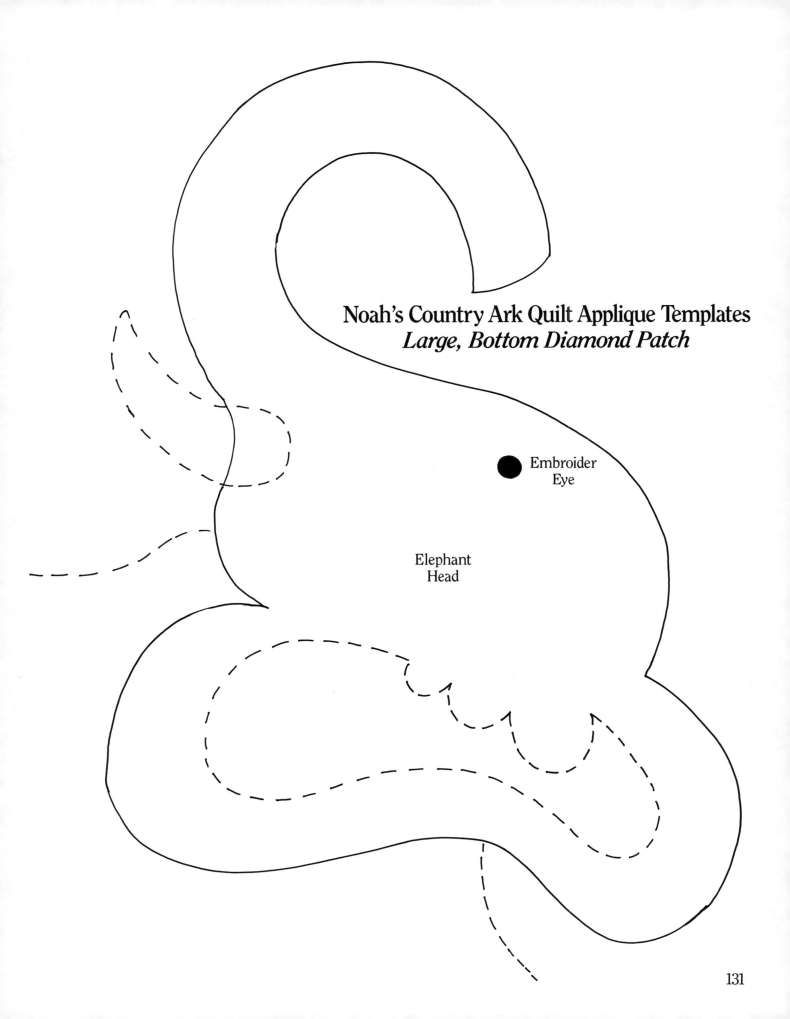

Noah's Country Ark Quilt Applique Templates
Large, Bottom Diamond Patch

Embroider
Eye

Elephant
Head

Noah's Country Ark Quilt Applique Templates
Large, Bottom Diamond Patch

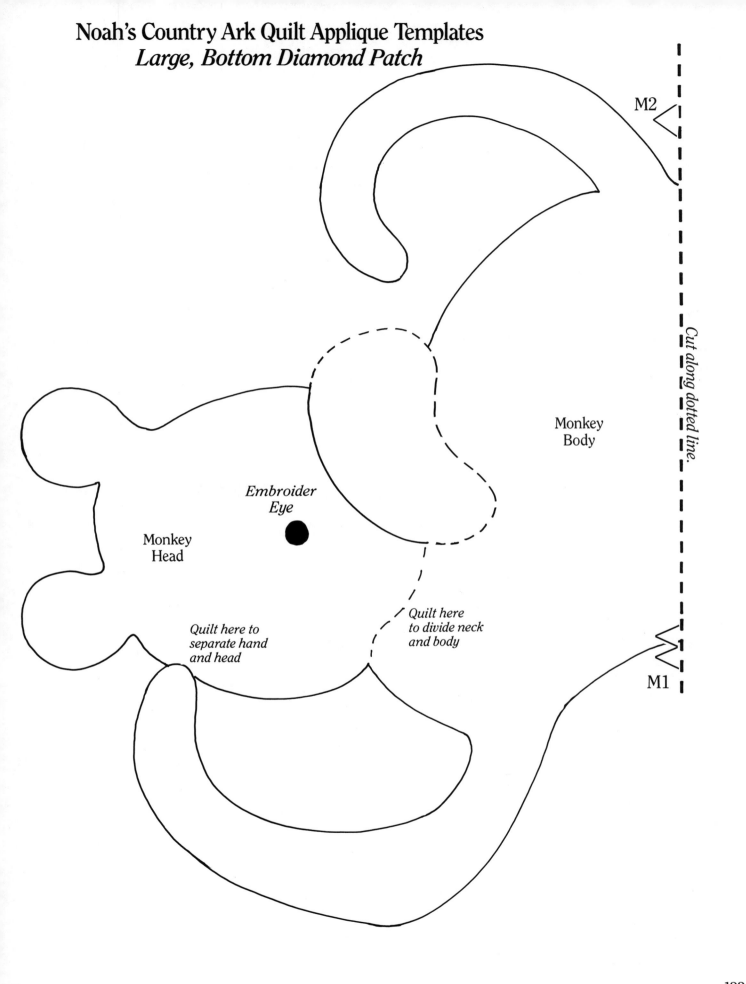

M2

Cut along dotted line.

Monkey Body

Embroider Eye

Monkey Head

Quilt here to separate hand and head

Quilt here to divide neck and body

M1

Noah's Country Ark Quilt Applique Templates
Large, Bottom Diamond Patch

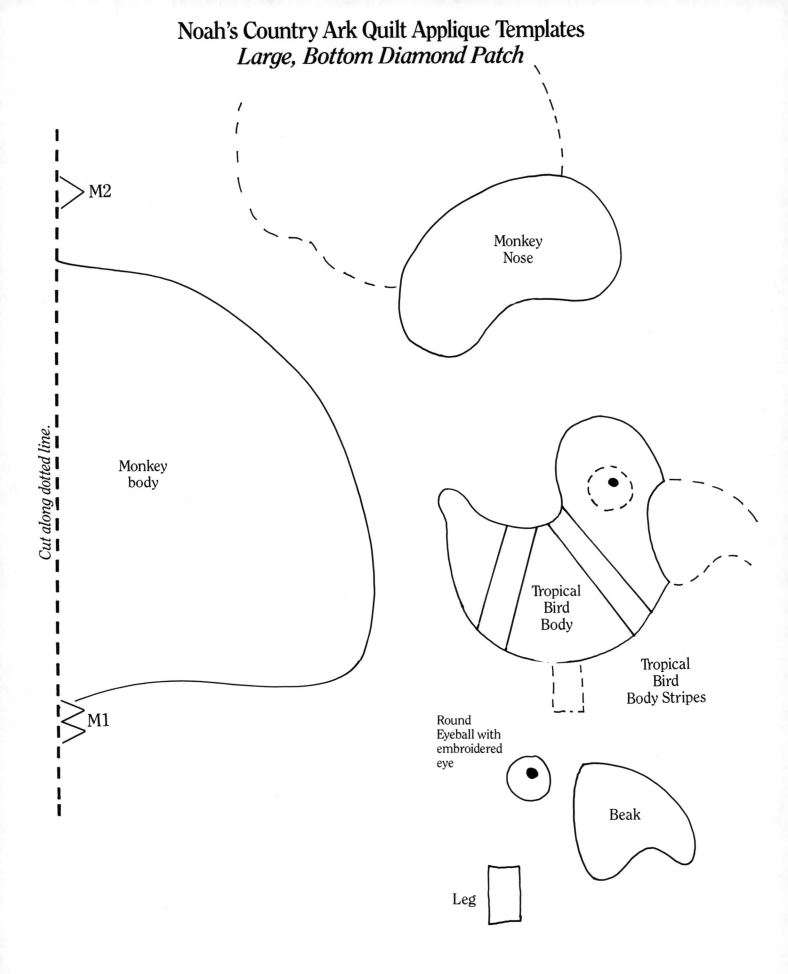

M2

Cut along dotted line.

Monkey Nose

Monkey body

Tropical Bird Body

Tropical Bird Body Stripes

M1

Round Eyeball with embroidered eye

Beak

Leg

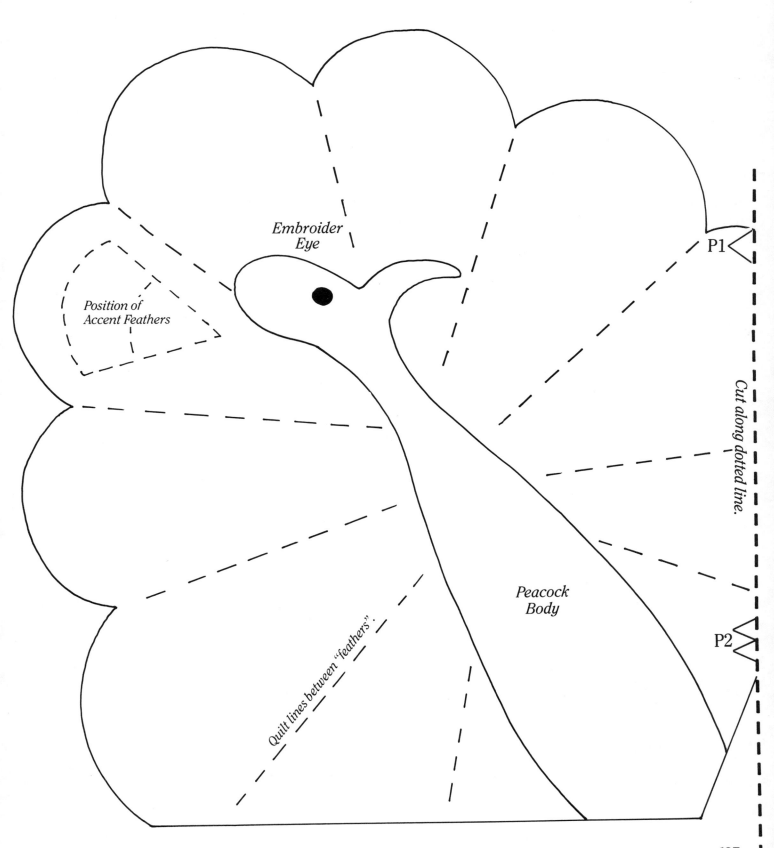

Embroider
Eye

Position of
Accent Feathers

P1

Cut along dotted line.

Quilt lines between "feathers".

Peacock
Body

P2

Noah's Country Ark Quilt Applique Templates
Large, Bottom Diamond Patch

Note: Porcupine Accents Ⓐ and Ⓑ should be cut from the same fabric.

P1

Cut along dotted line.

Porcupine Accent Ⓐ

Porcupine Accent ①

P2

Porcupine Accent Ⓑ

Porcupine Accent ②

Note: Porcupine Accents ① and ② should be cut from the same fabric.

Porcupine Head

Embroider Eye

Back Paw

Front Paw

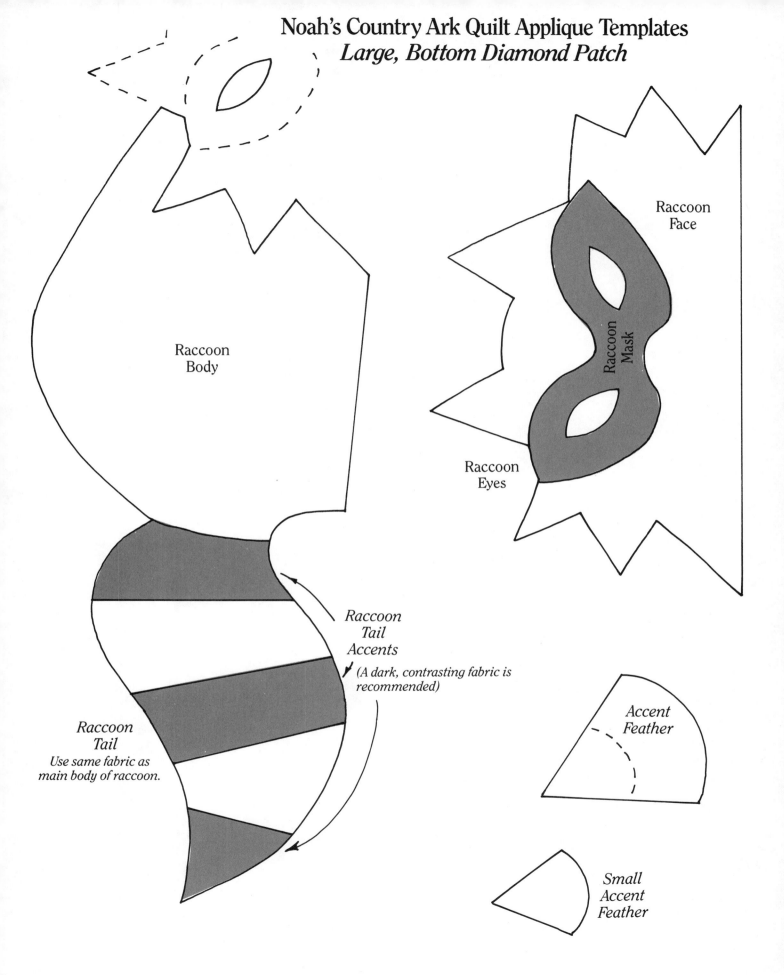

Raccoon
Body

Raccoon
Face

Raccoon
Mask

Raccoon
Eyes

*Raccoon
Tail
Accents*

*(A dark, contrasting fabric is
recommended)*

*Raccoon
Tail*
*Use same fabric as
main body of raccoon.*

*Accent
Feather*

*Small
Accent
Feather*

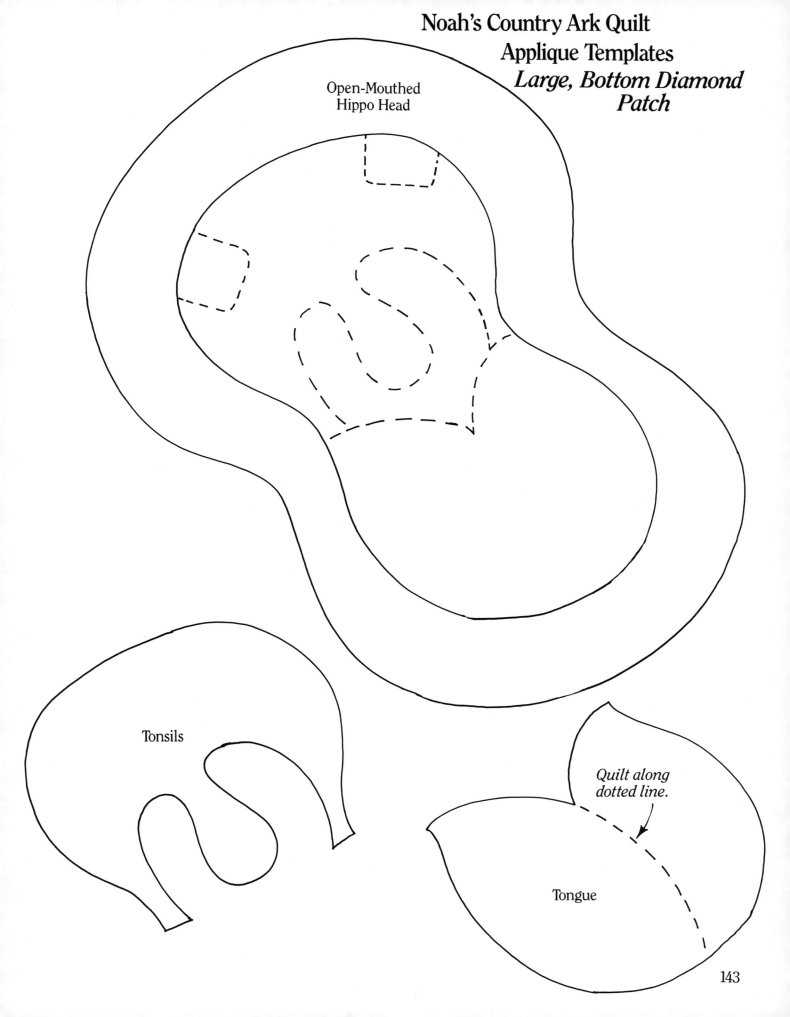

Noah's Country Ark Quilt
Applique Templates
Large, Bottom Diamond Patch

Open-Mouthed
Hippo Head

Tonsils

Quilt along dotted line.

Tongue

143

Noah's Country Ark Quilt Applique Templates
Large, Bottom Diamond Patch

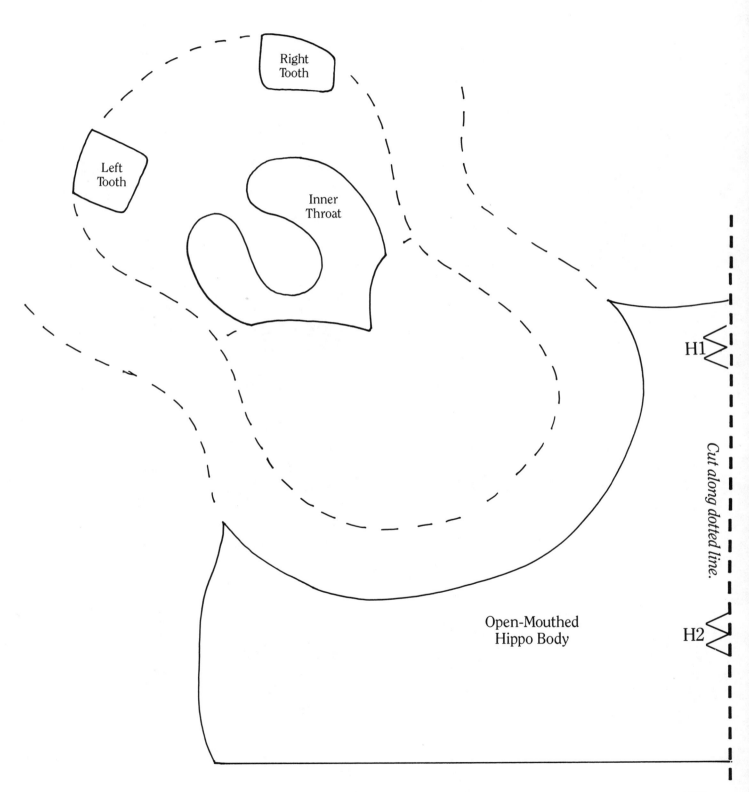

Right
Tooth

Left
Tooth

Inner
Throat

H1

H2

Open-Mouthed
Hippo Body

Cut along dotted line.

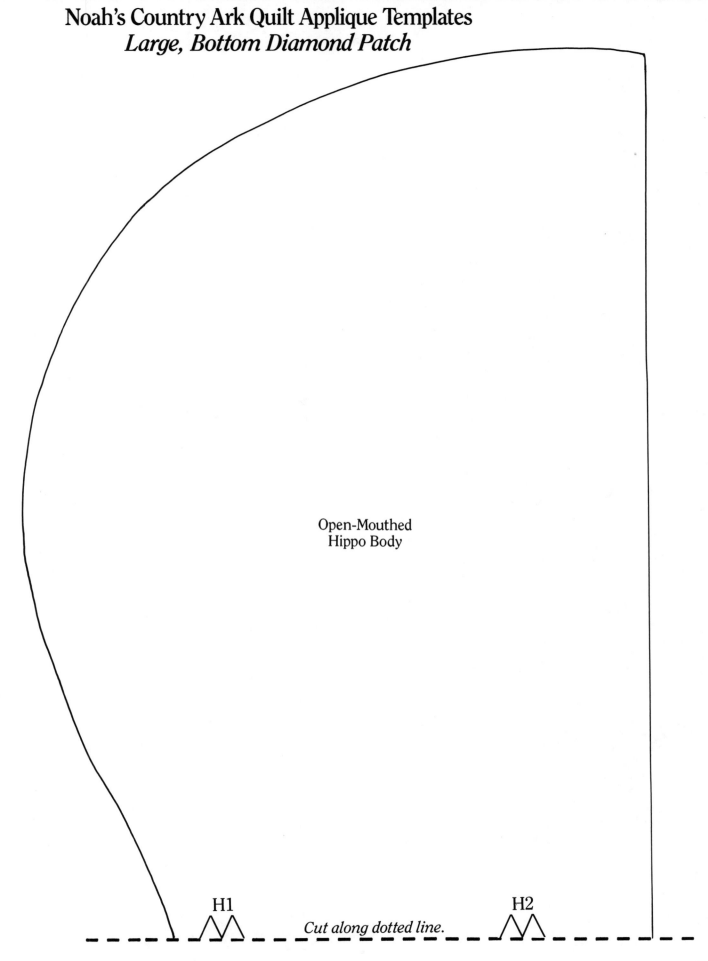

Open-Mouthed
Hippo Body

H1

H2

Cut along dotted line.

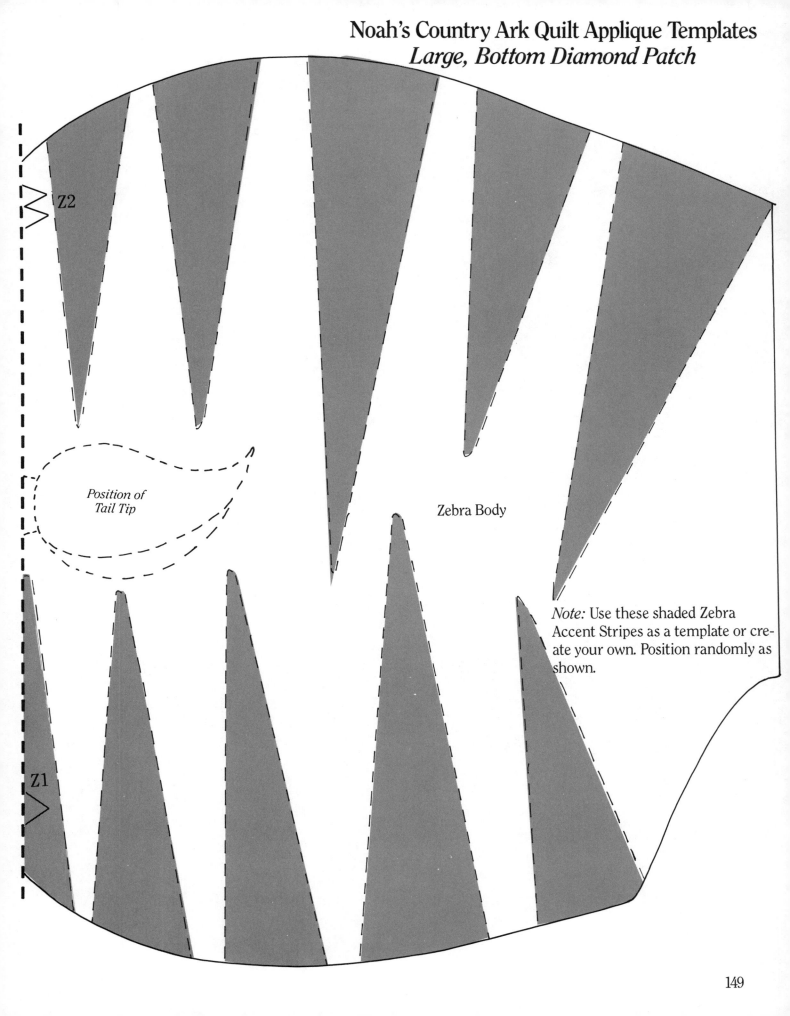

Z2

*Position of
Tail Tip*

Zebra Body

Note: Use these shaded Zebra Accent Stripes as a template or create your own. Position randomly as shown.

Z1

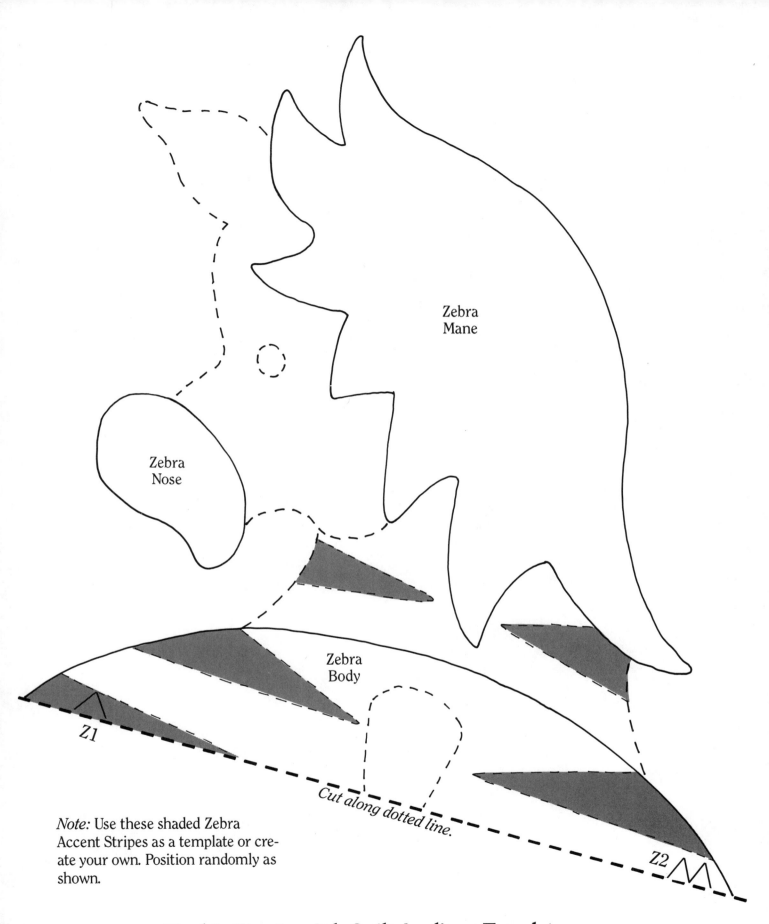

Zebra
Mane

Zebra
Nose

Zebra
Body

Z1

Z2

Cut along dotted line.

Note: Use these shaded Zebra
Accent Stripes as a template or create your own. Position randomly as
shown.

Noah's Country Ark Quilt Applique Templates
Large, Bottom Diamond Patch

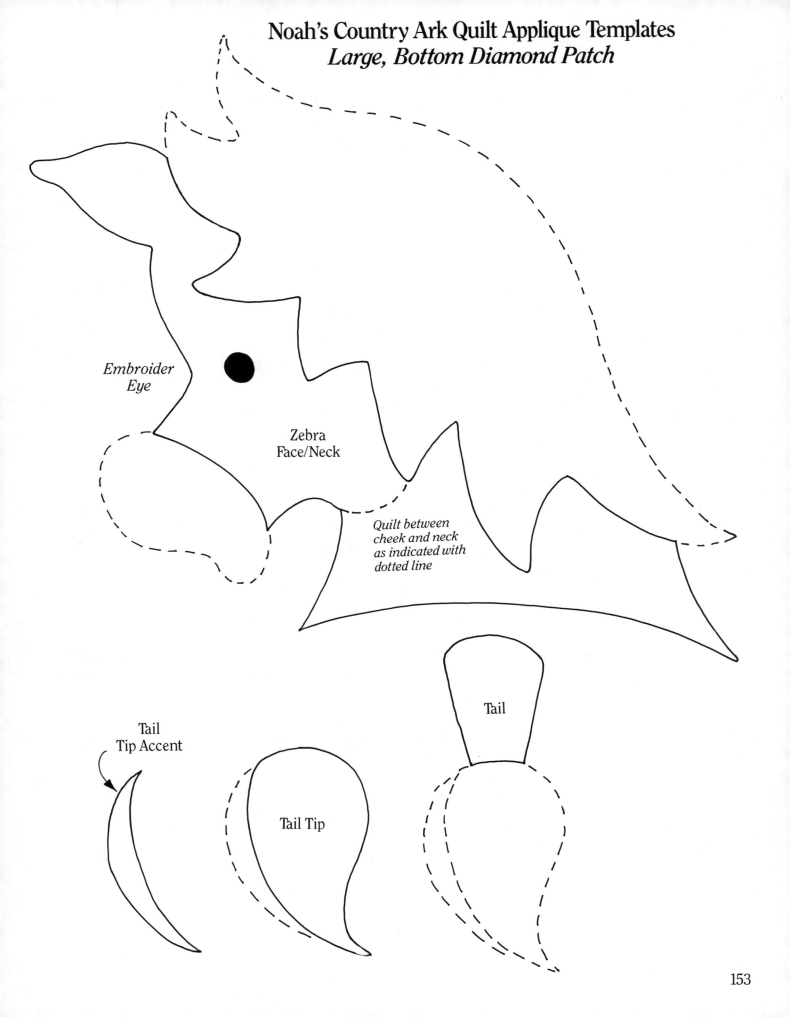

Noah's Country Ark Quilt Applique Templates
Large, Bottom Diamond Patch

Embroider Eye

Zebra
Face/Neck

Quilt between cheek and neck as indicated with dotted line

Tail

Tail
Tip Accent

Tail Tip

153

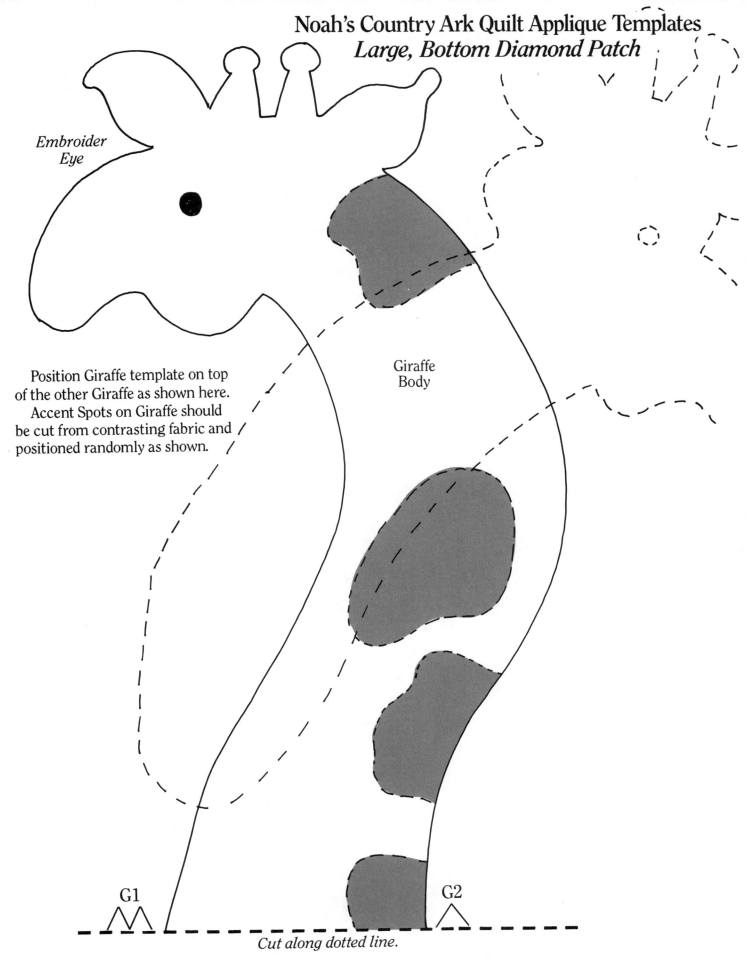

Embroider Eye

Position Giraffe template on top of the other Giraffe as shown here. Accent Spots on Giraffe should be cut from contrasting fabric and positioned randomly as shown.

Giraffe Body

G1

G2

Cut along dotted line.

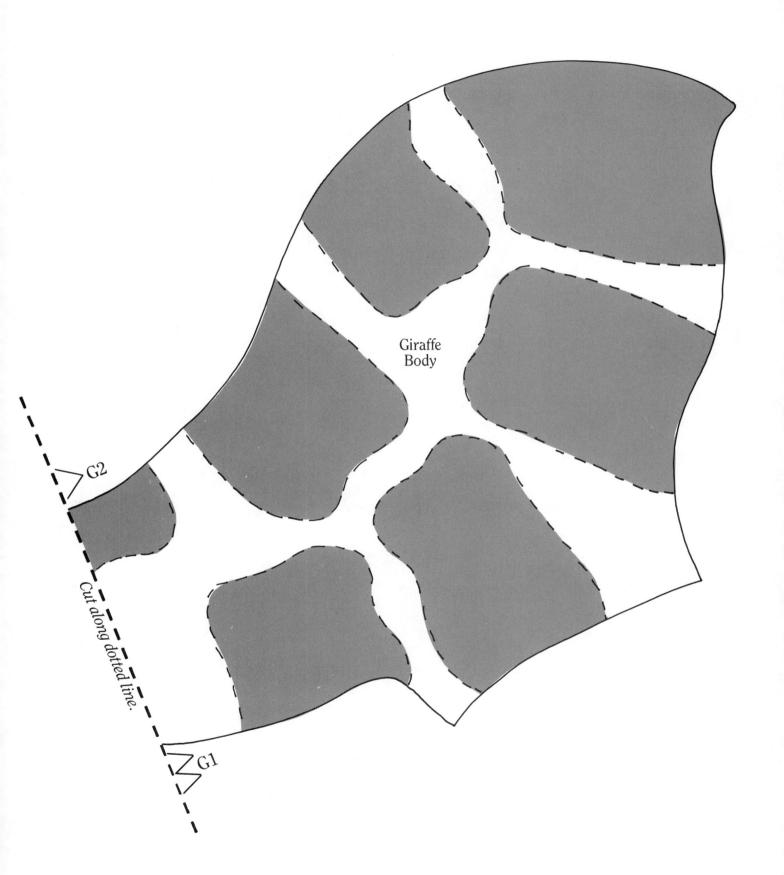

Giraffe
Body

G2

Cut along dotted line.

G1

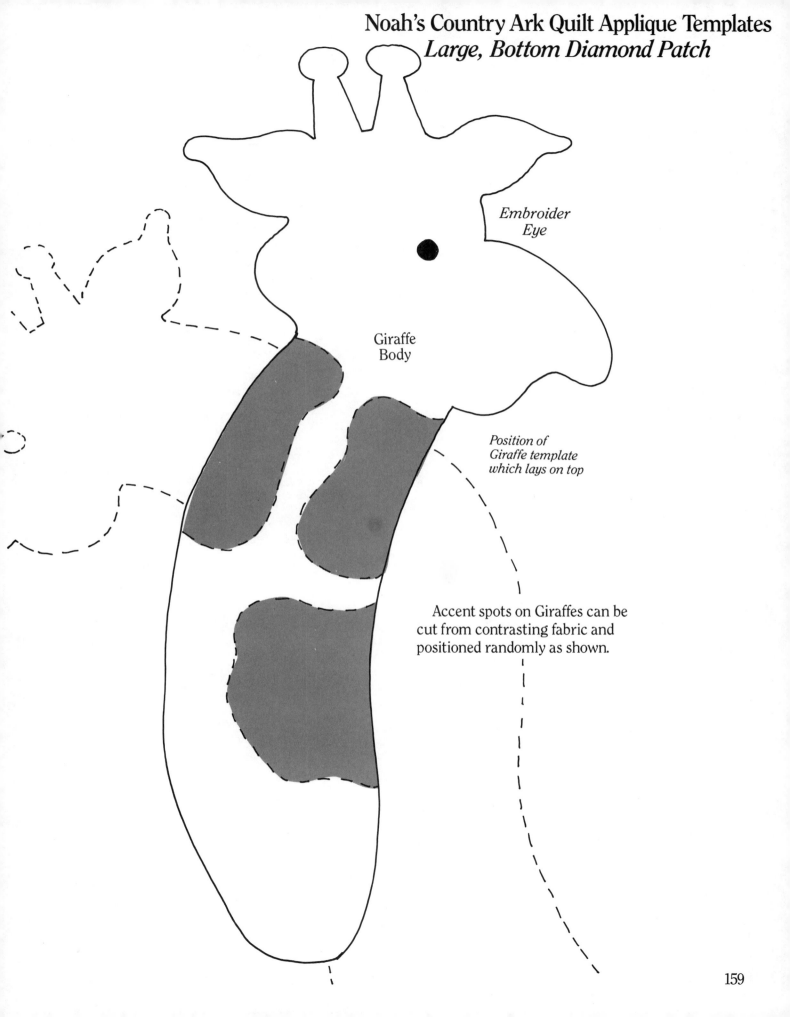

Embroider Eye

Giraffe Body

Position of Giraffe template which lays on top

Accent spots on Giraffes can be cut from contrasting fabric and positioned randomly as shown.

Noah's Country Ark Quilt Applique Layout
Winding Vine

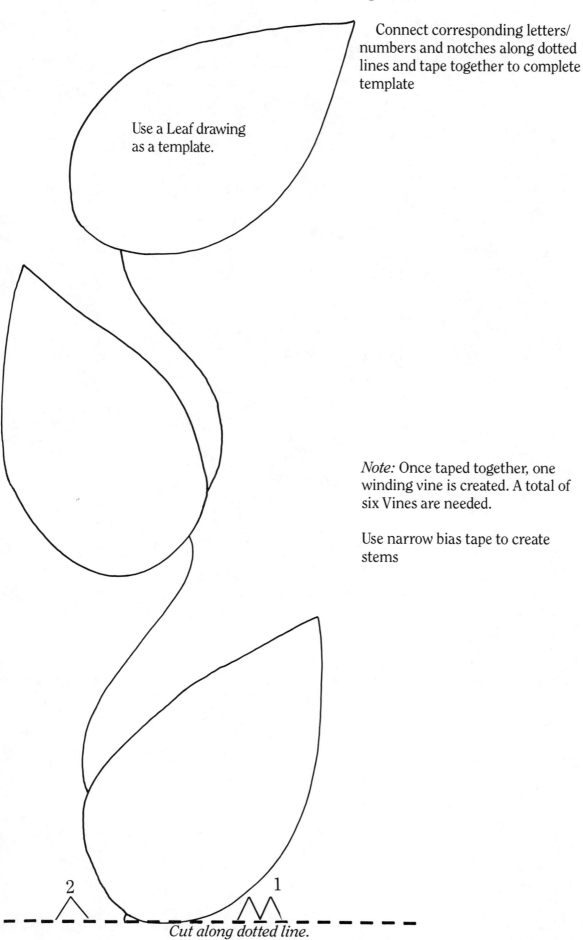

Connect corresponding letters/
numbers and notches along dotted
lines and tape together to complete
template

Use a Leaf drawing
as a template.

Note: Once taped together, one
winding vine is created. A total of
six Vines are needed.

Use narrow bias tape to create
stems

2

1

Cut along dotted line.

Noah's Country Ark Quilt Applique Layout
Winding Vine

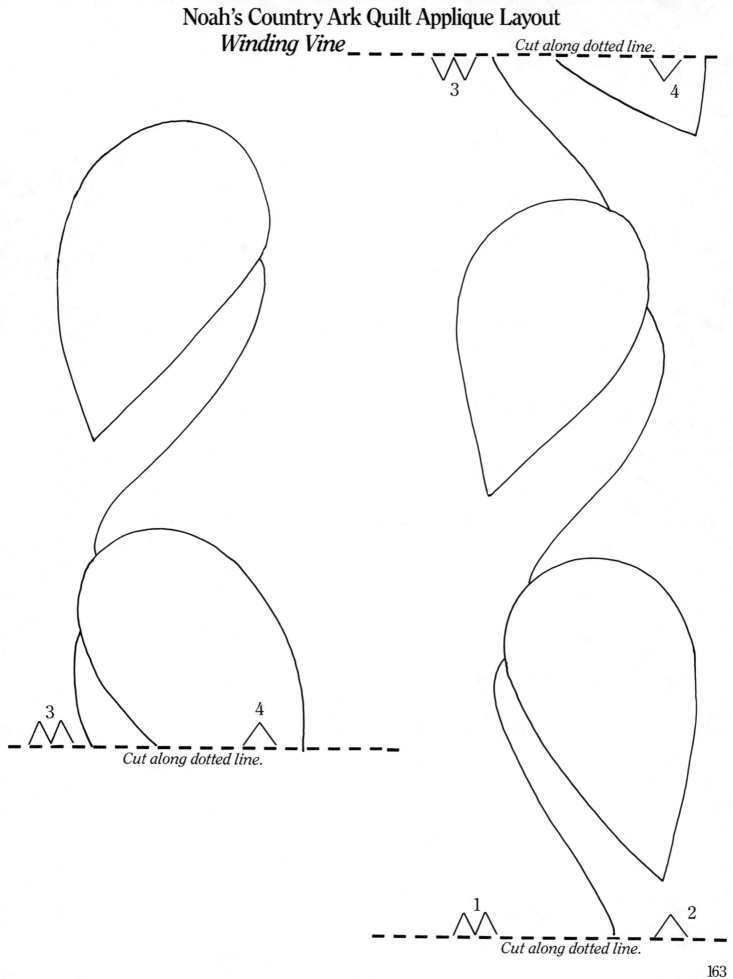

Cut along dotted line.

3

4

3

4

Cut along dotted line.

1

2

Cut along dotted line.

Noah's Country Ark Quilt Quilting and Piecing Layout
Corner Triangle Patches

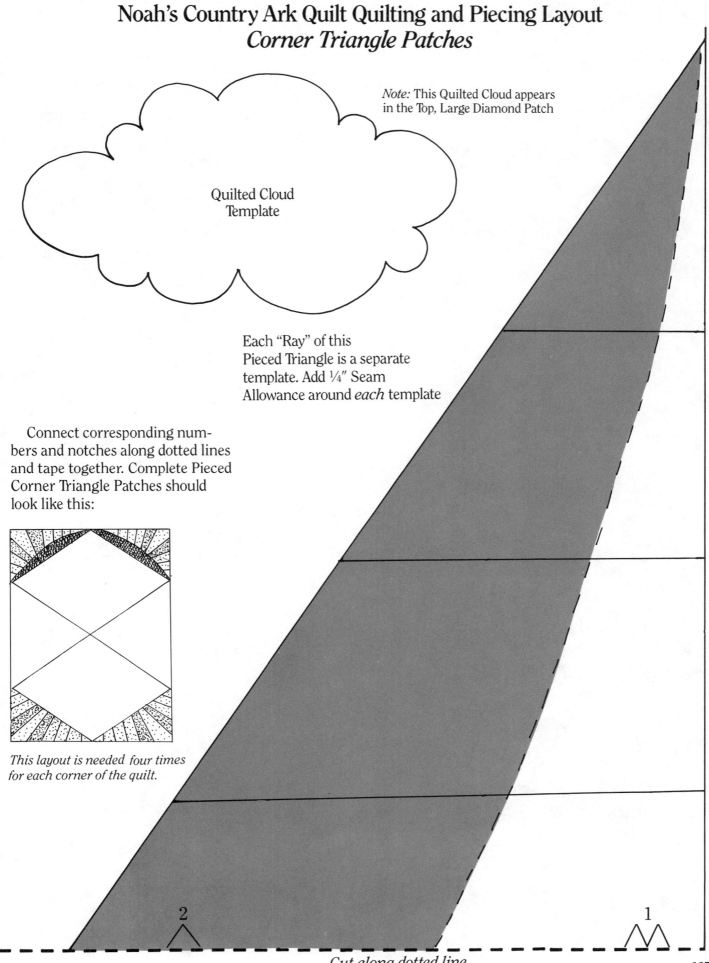

Quilted Cloud
Template

Note: This Quilted Cloud appears
in the Top, Large Diamond Patch

Each "Ray" of this
Pieced Triangle is a separate
template. Add ¼″ Seam
Allowance around *each* template

Connect corresponding numbers and notches along dotted lines
and tape together. Complete Pieced
Corner Triangle Patches should
look like this:

*This layout is needed four times
for each corner of the quilt.*

2

1

Cut along dotted line.

Noah's Country Ark Quilt Quilting and Piecing Layout
Corner Triangle Patches

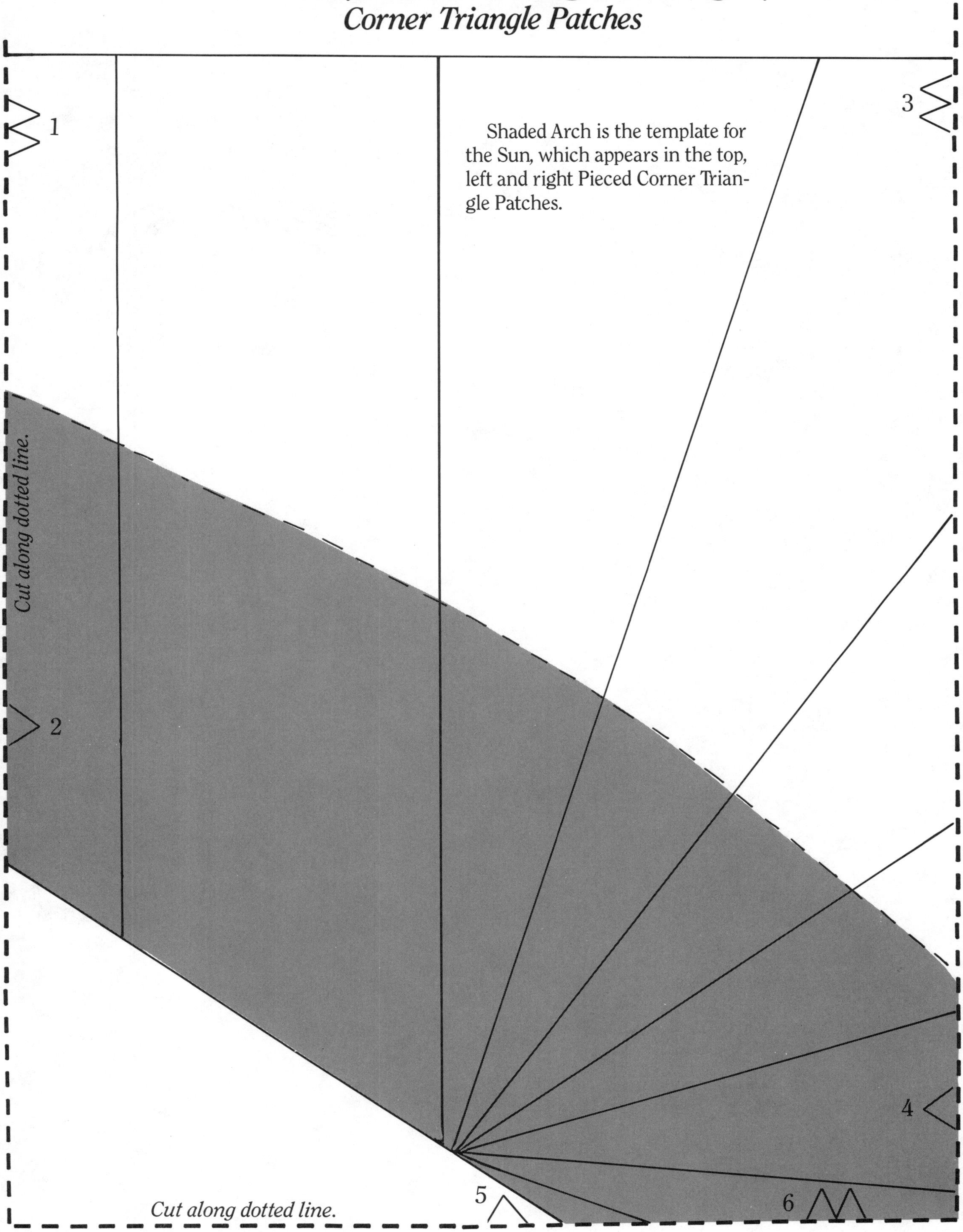
Shaded Arch is the template for the Sun, which appears in the top, left and right Pieced Corner Triangle Patches.
1
2
3
4
5
6
Cut along dotted line.
Cut along dotted line.

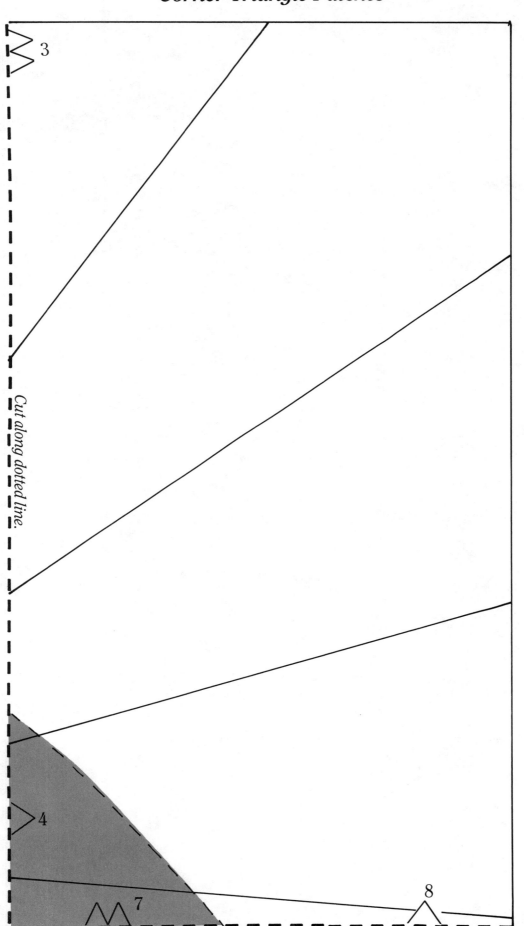

Cut along dotted line.

3

4

7

8

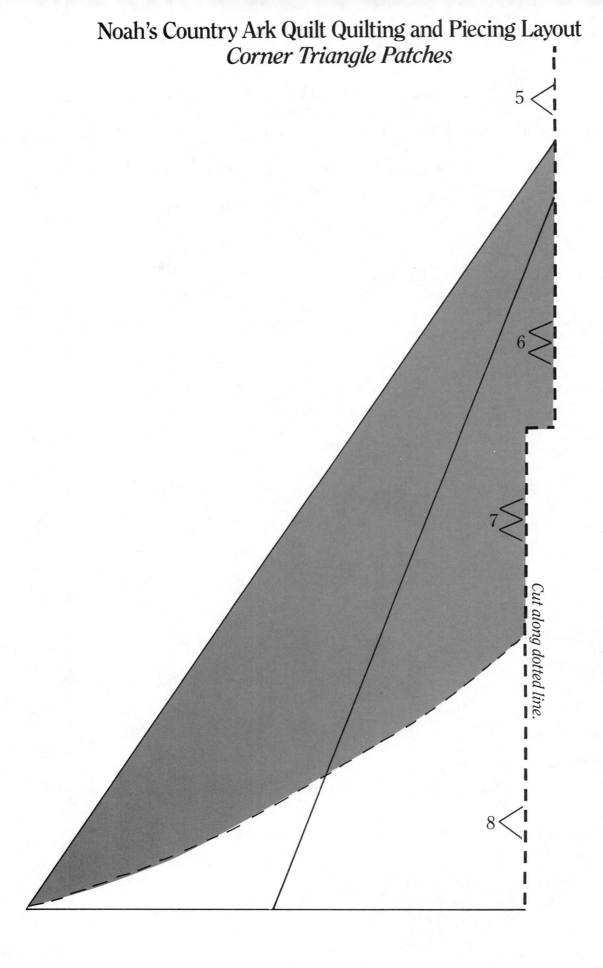

5

6

7

Cut along dotted line.

8

172

The Country Circus Quilt Applique Layout
Center Diamond Patch

To create the finished layout, match corresponding letters/numbers and notches along dotted lines and tape together. Complete Applique Layout will look like this:

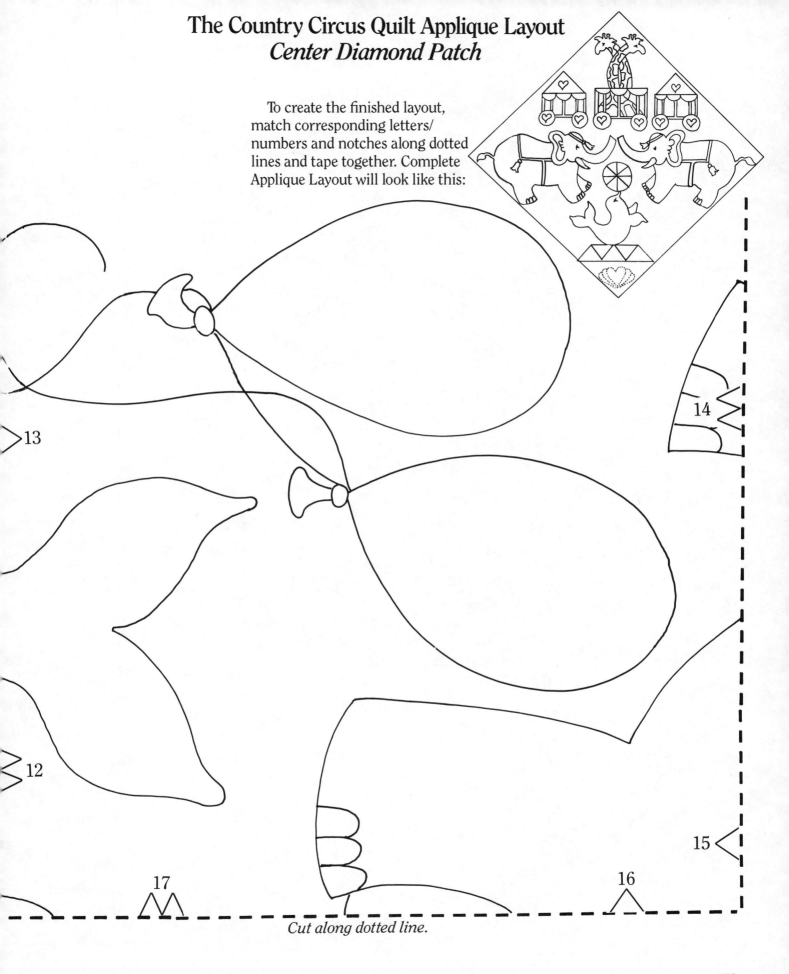

13

14

12

15

17

16

Cut along dotted line.

The Country Circus Quilt Applique Layout
Center Diamond Patch

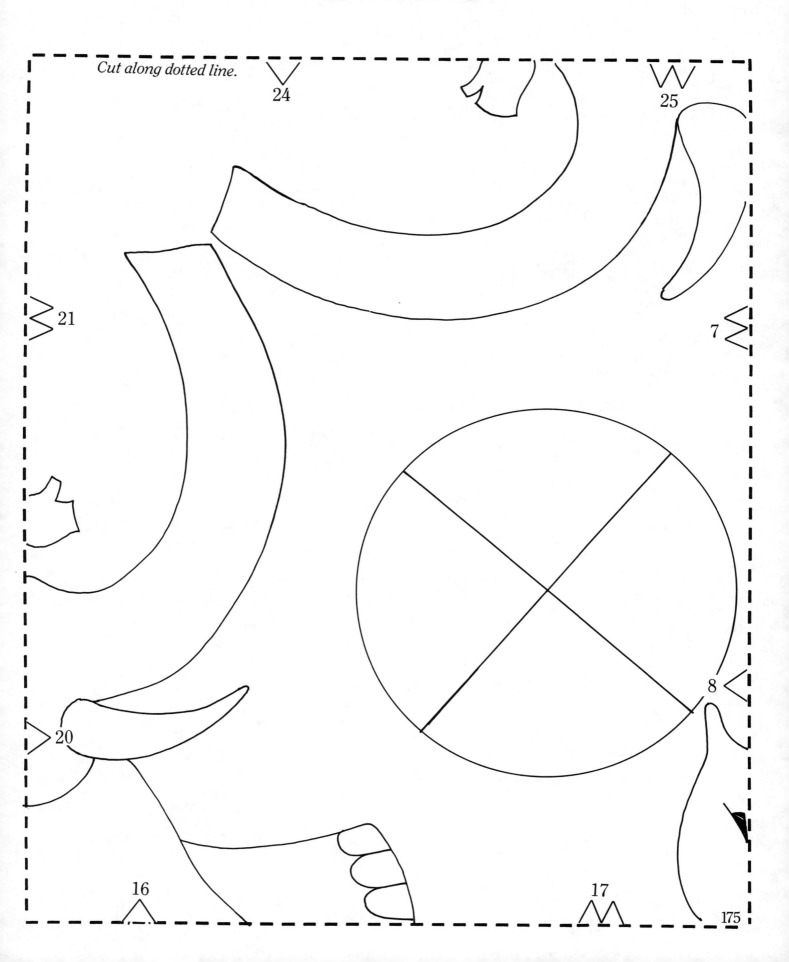

Cut along dotted line.

24

25

21

7

20

8

16

17

175

Cut along dotted line.

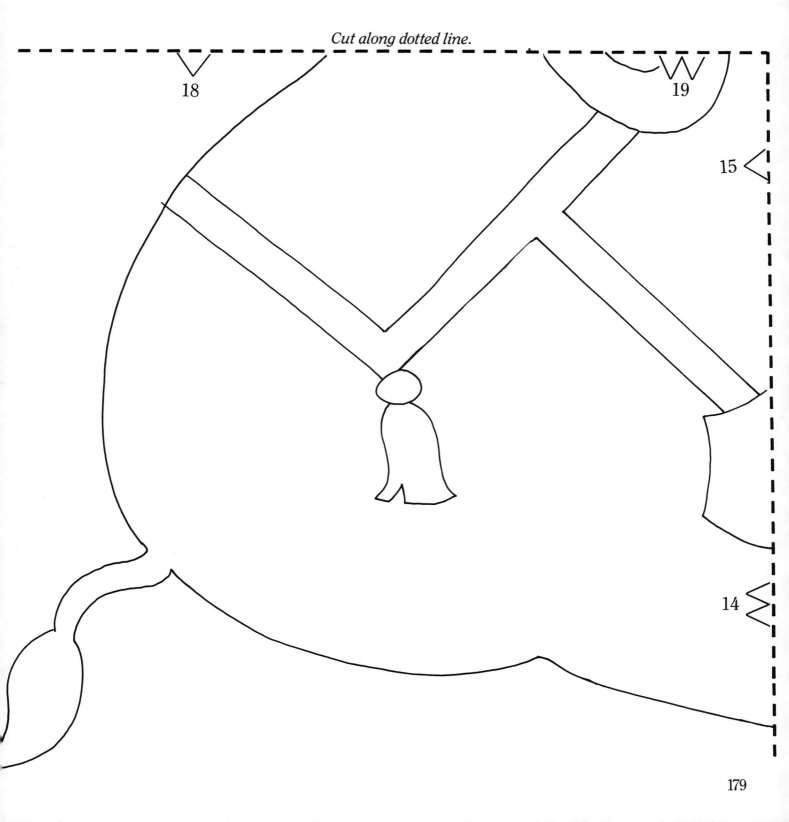

Cut along dotted line.

18

19

15

14

11

10

9

12

13

Cut along dotted line.

Cut along dotted line.

The Country Circus Quilt Applique Layout
Center Diamond Patch

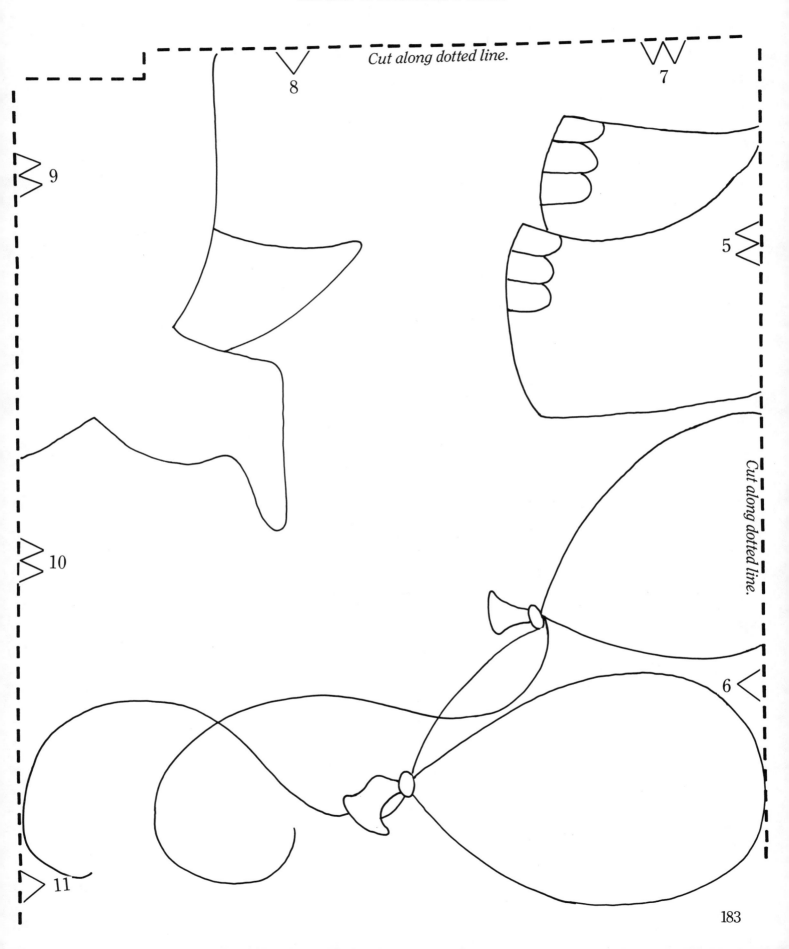

Cut along dotted line.

8

7

9

5

Cut along dotted line.

10

6

11

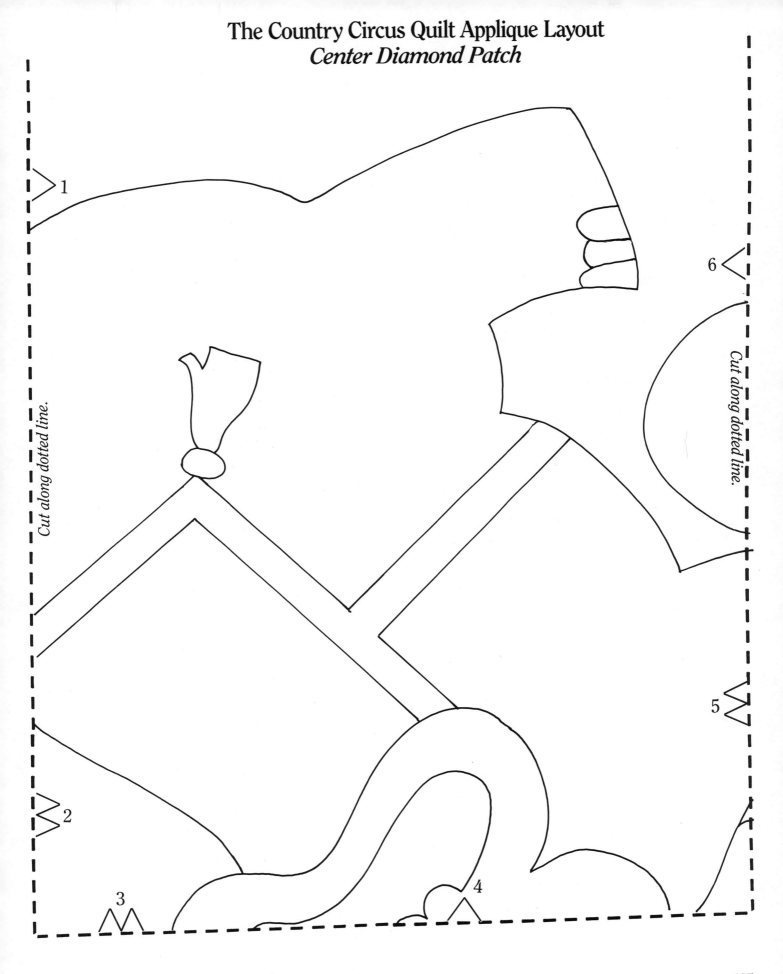

Cut along dotted line.

Cut along dotted line.

The Country Circus Quilt Applique Layout
Center Diamond Patch

Cut along dotted line.

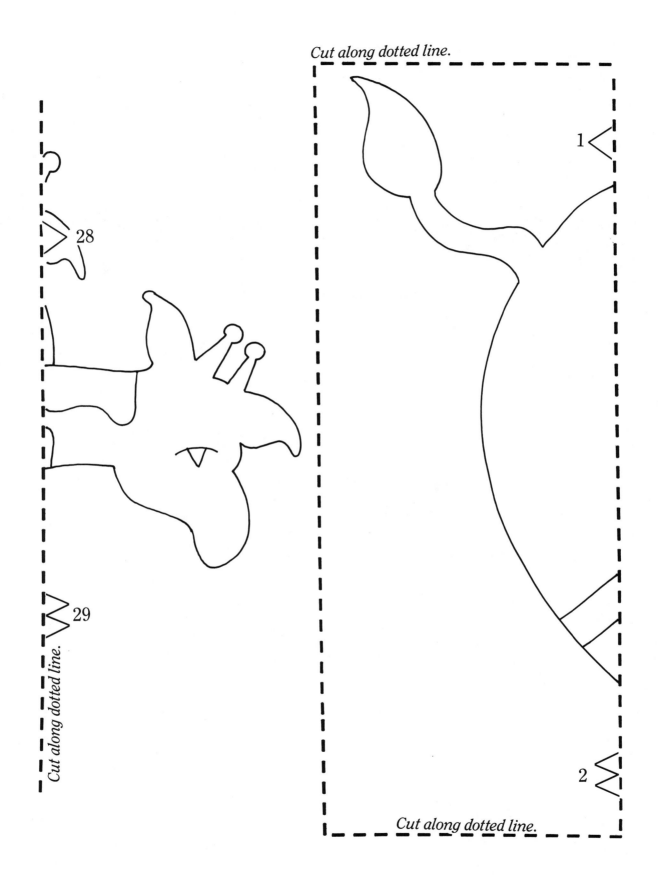

1

28

Cut along dotted line.

29

2

Cut along dotted line.

Cut along dotted line.

The Country Circus Quilt Applique Templates
Center Diamond Patch

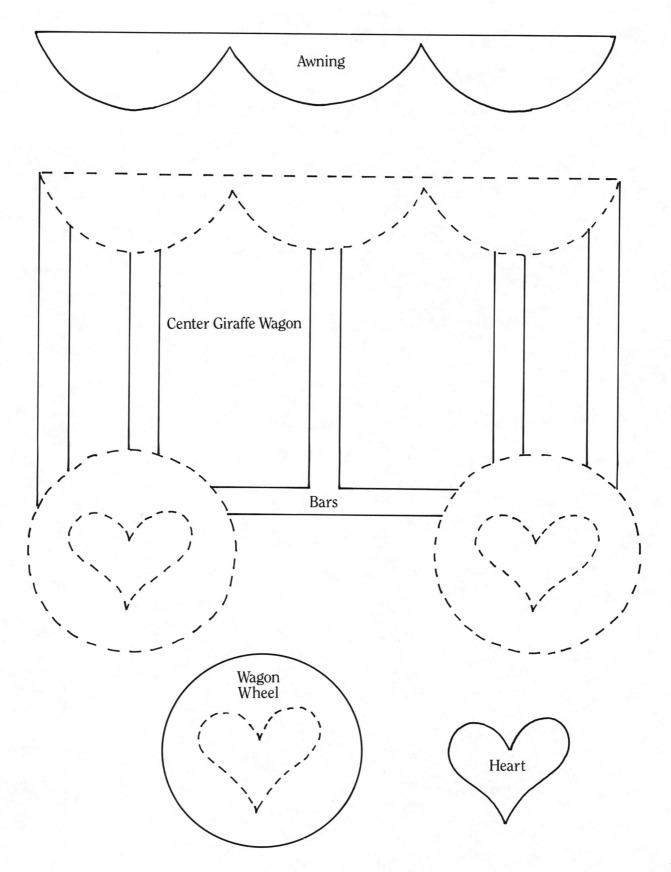

Awning

Center Giraffe Wagon

Bars

Wagon
Wheel

Heart

The Small Circus Wagon appears twice on Center Diamond Patch and is also centered on each of the four Small Square Patches.

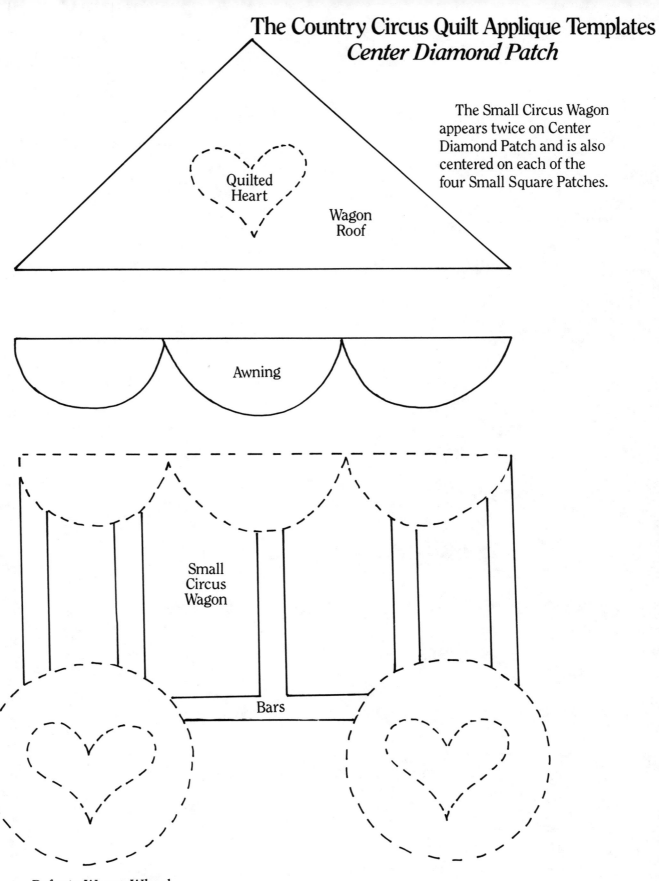

Quilted Heart

Wagon Roof

Awning

Small Circus Wagon

Bars

Refer to Wagon Wheel template on previous page.

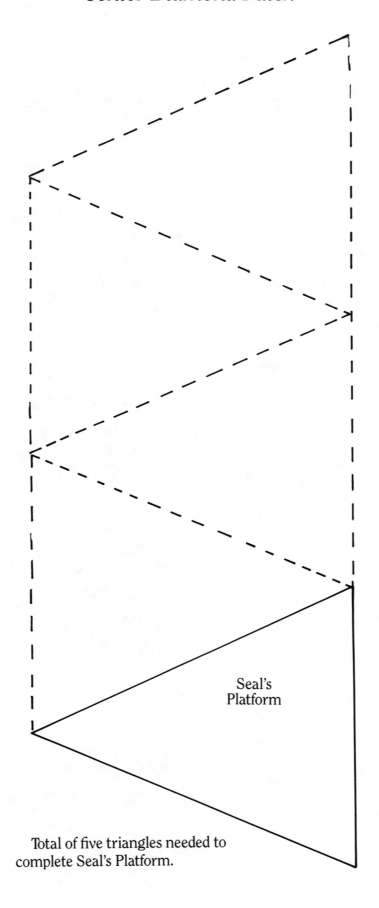

Seal's
Platform

Total of five triangles needed to
complete Seal's Platform.

The Country Circus Quilt Applique Templates
Center Diamond Patch

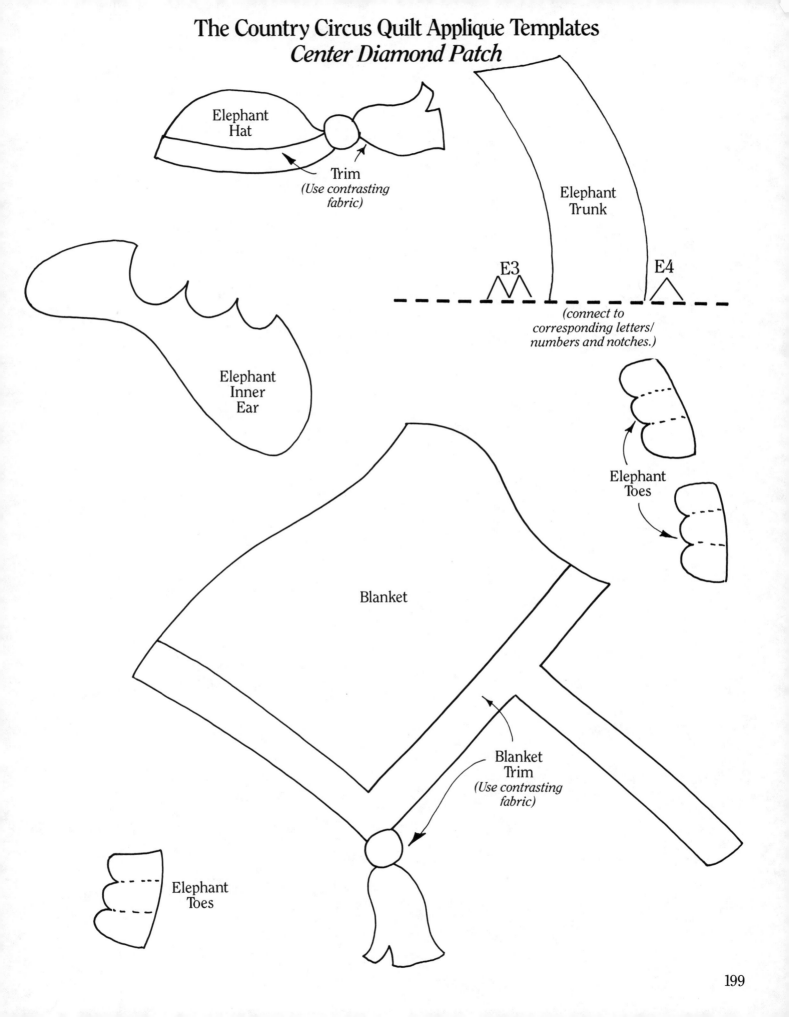

Elephant
Hat

Trim
*(Use contrasting
fabric)*

Elephant
Trunk

E3

E4

*(connect to
corresponding letters/
numbers and notches.)*

Elephant
Inner
Ear

Elephant
Toes

Blanket

Blanket
Trim
*(Use contrasting
fabric)*

Elephant
Toes

The Country Circus Quilt Applique Templates
Center Diamond Patch

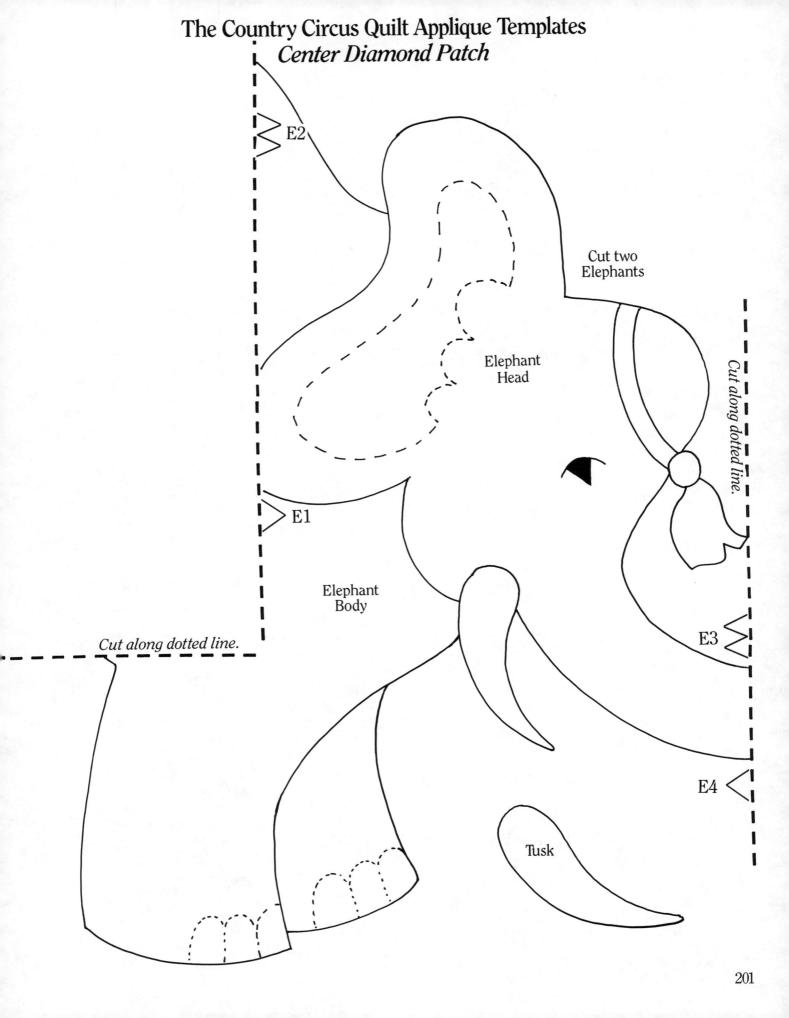

E2

Cut two
Elephants

Cut along dotted line.

Elephant
Head

E1

Cut along dotted line.

Elephant
Body

E3

Tusk

E4

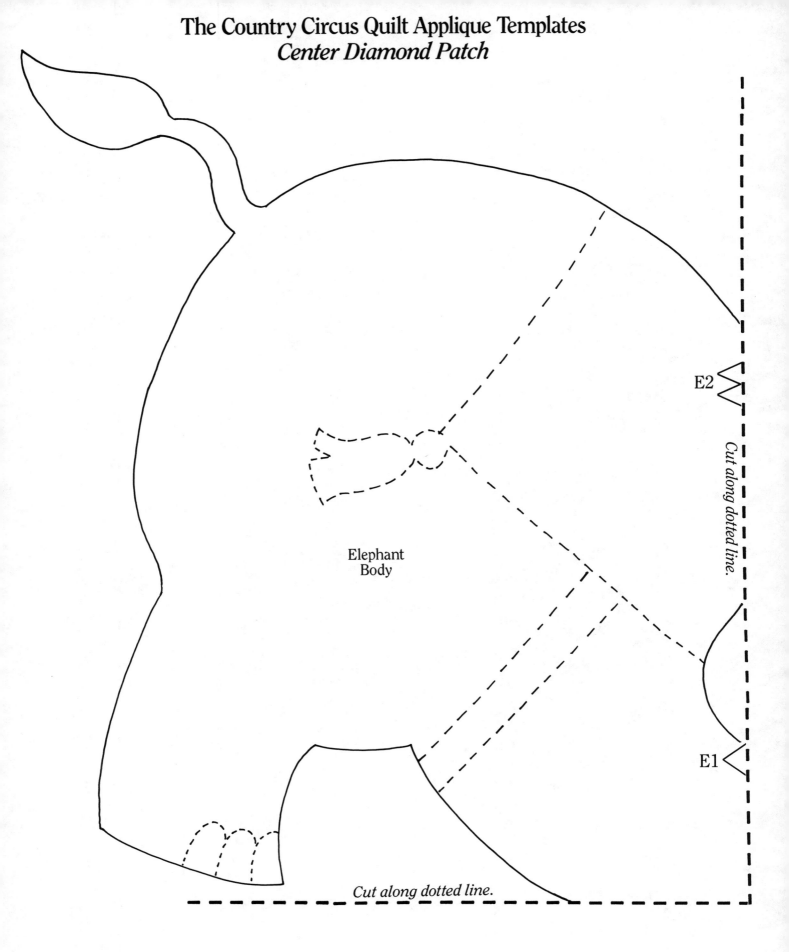

Elephant
Body

E2

E1

Cut along dotted line.

Cut along dotted line.

The Country Circus Quilt Applique Templates
Center Diamond Patch

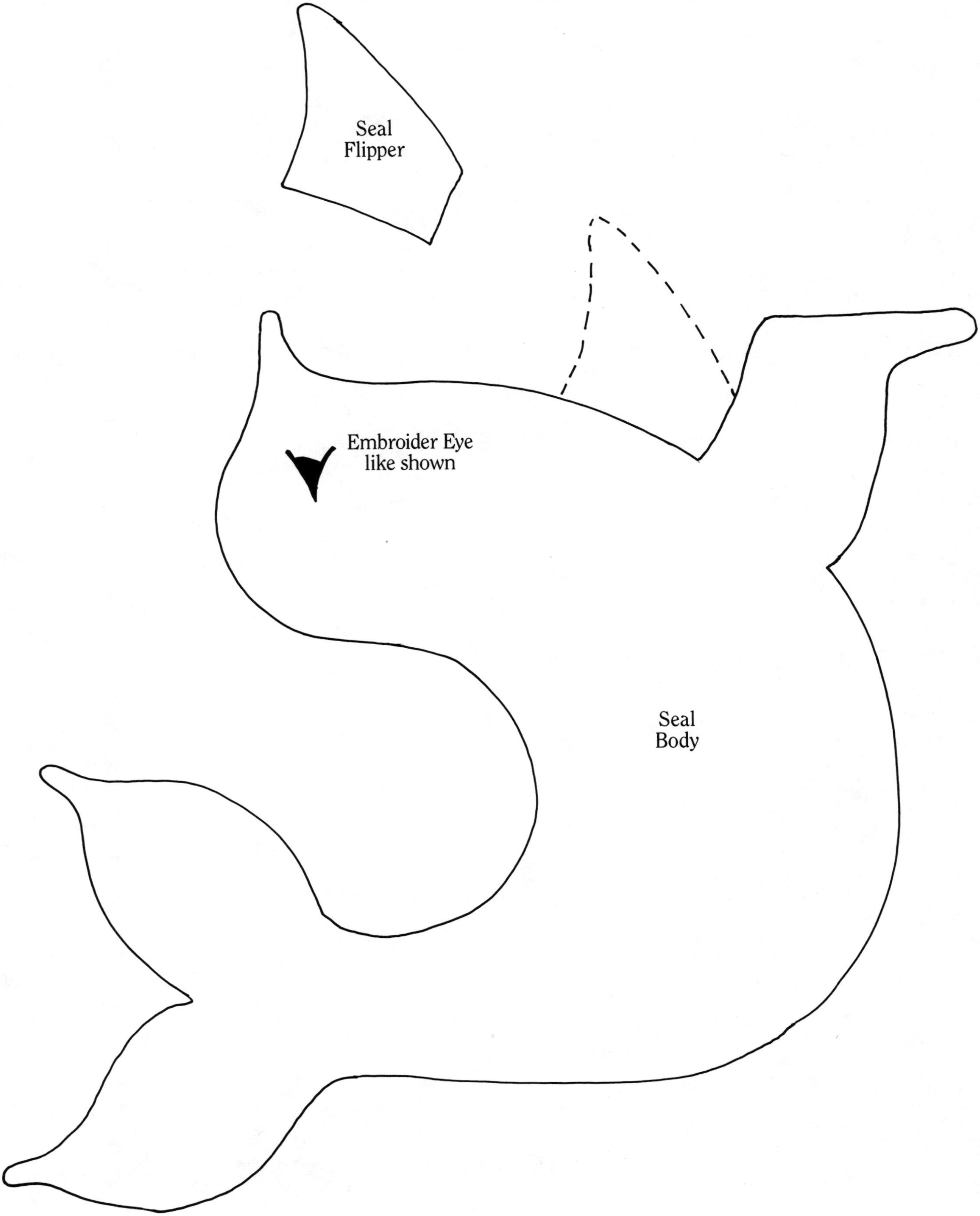
Seal
Flipper
Embroider Eye
like shown
Seal
Body

The Country Circus Quilt Applique Templates
Center Diamond Patch

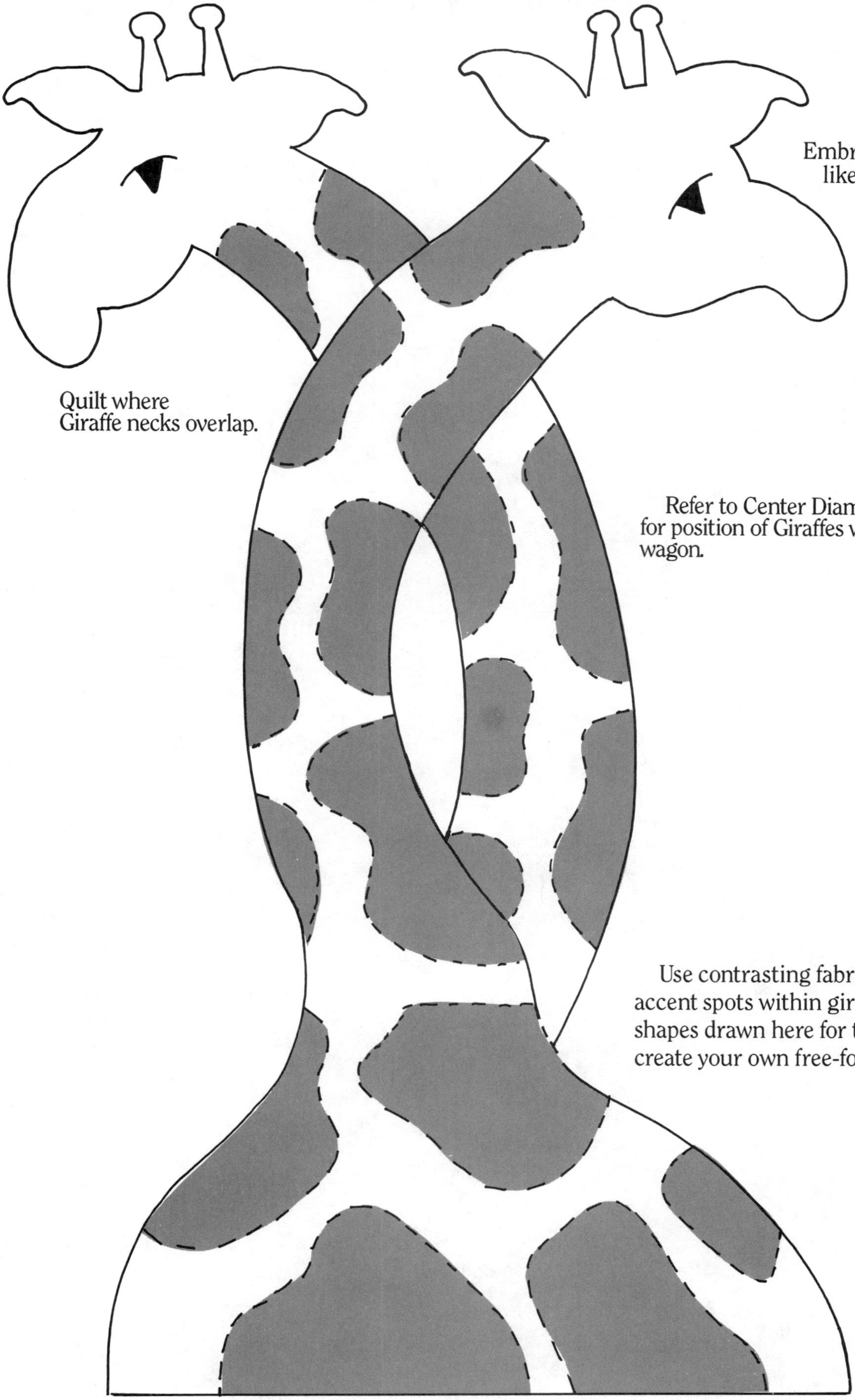

Embroider Eye
like shown

Quilt where
Giraffe necks overlap.

Refer to Center Diamond Layout
for position of Giraffes within
wagon.

Use contrasting fabric to create
accent spots within giraffes. Use
shapes drawn here for templates or
create your own free-form shapes.

The Country Circus Quilt Applique Layout
Small Patch

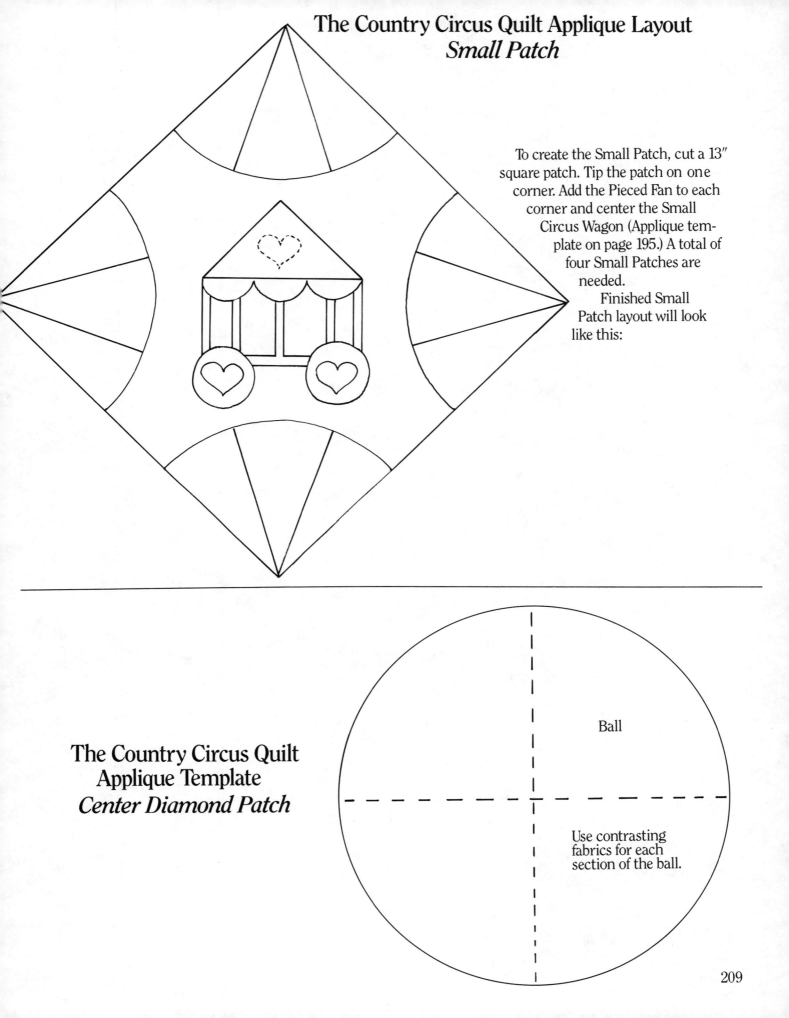

To create the Small Patch, cut a 13″ square patch. Tip the patch on one corner. Add the Pieced Fan to each corner and center the Small Circus Wagon (Applique template on page 195.) A total of four Small Patches are needed.

Finished Small Patch layout will look like this:

The Country Circus Quilt Applique Template
Center Diamond Patch

Ball

Use contrasting fabrics for each section of the ball.

The Country Circus Quilt
Piecing Templates
Small Patch Fan

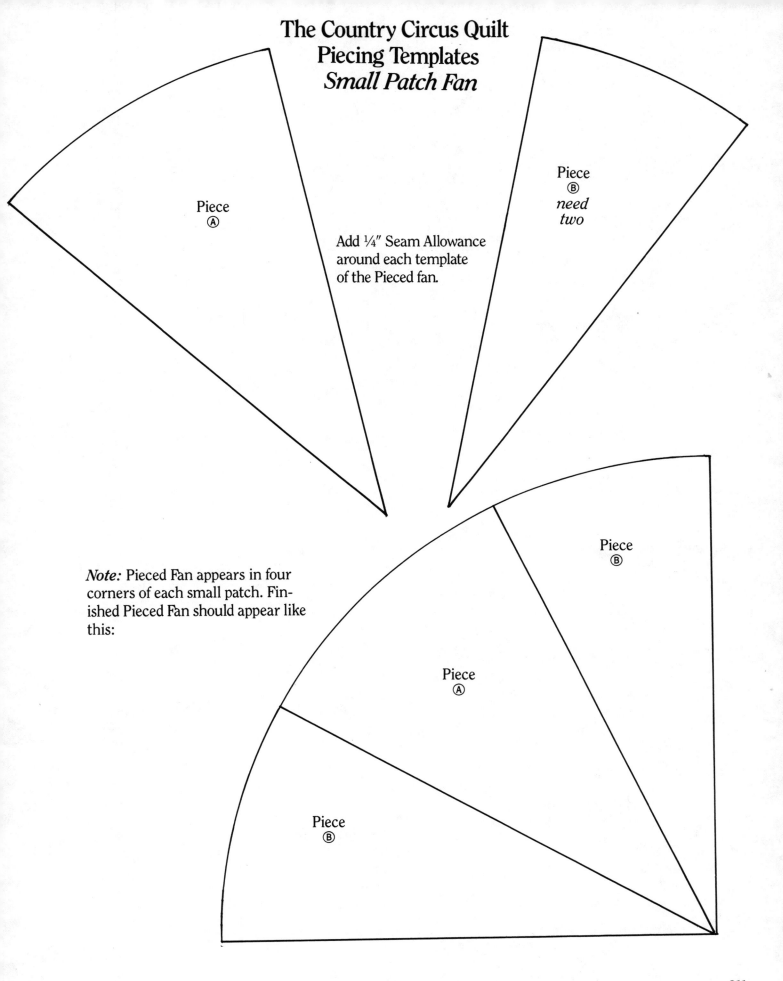

Piece
Ⓐ

Piece
Ⓑ
*need
two*

Add ¼″ Seam Allowance
around each template
of the Pieced fan.

Note: Pieced Fan appears in four
corners of each small patch. Finished Pieced Fan should appear like
this:

Piece
Ⓑ

Piece
Ⓐ

Piece
Ⓑ

The Country Circus Quilt Quilting Layout
Large Quilted Heart Triangle Patch

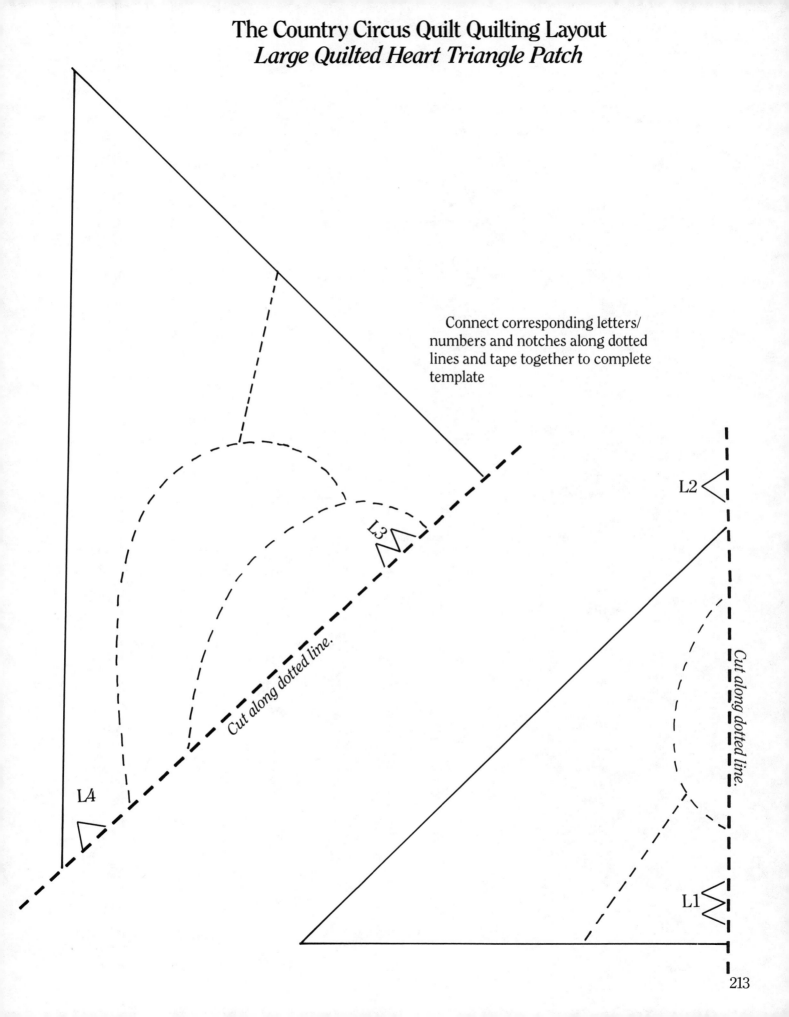

Connect corresponding letters/
numbers and notches along dotted
lines and tape together to complete
template

L2

L3

Cut along dotted line.

L4

L1

Cut along dotted line.

The Country Circus Quilt Quilting Layout
Large Quilted Heart Triangle Patch

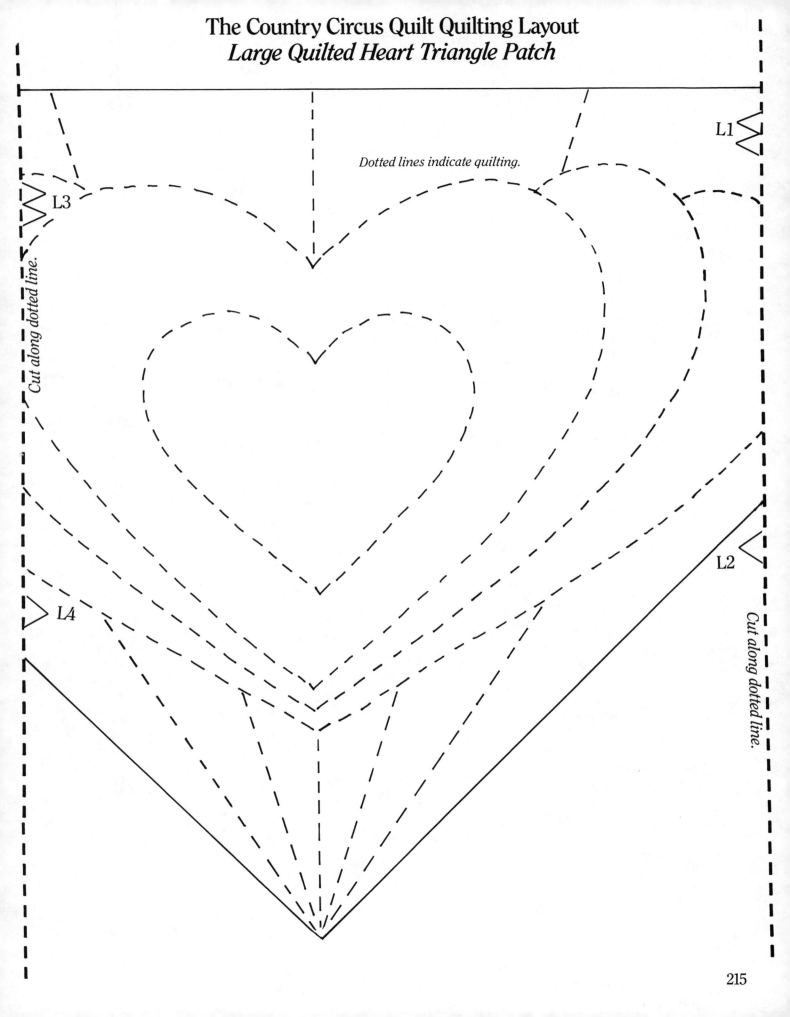

Dotted lines indicate quilting.

L1

L3

Cut along dotted line.

L2

L4

Cut along dotted line.

The Country Circus Quilt Quilting Layout
Small Quilted Heart Triangle Patch

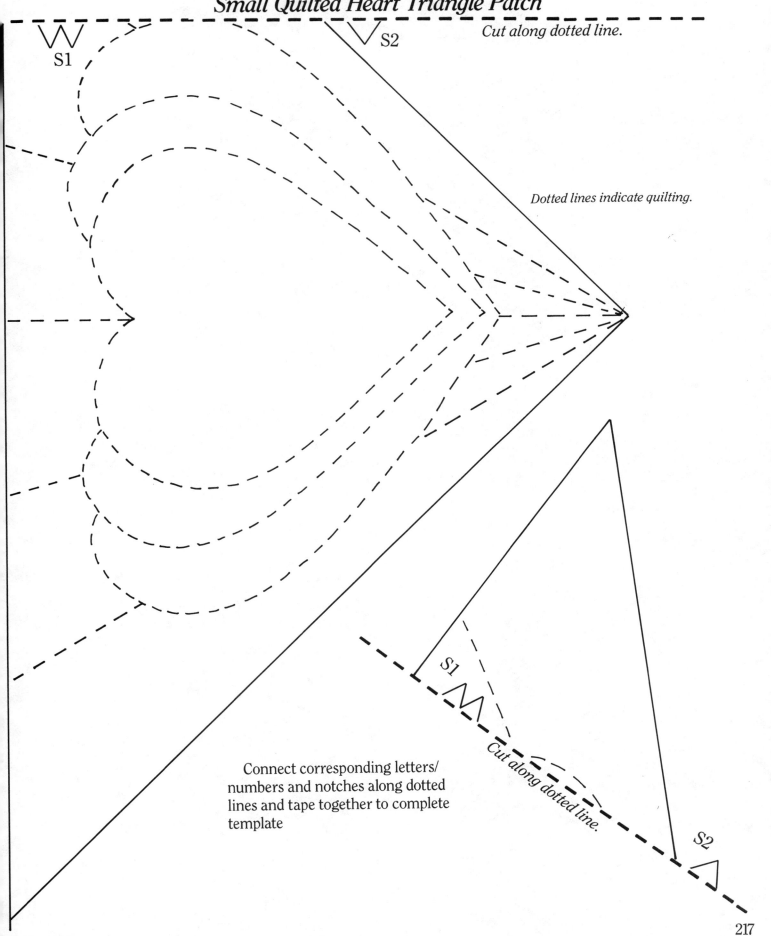

S1

S2

Cut along dotted line.

Dotted lines indicate quilting.

Connect corresponding letters/
numbers and notches along dotted
lines and tape together to complete
template

S1

Cut along dotted line.

S2

The Country Circus Quilt Pieced Border

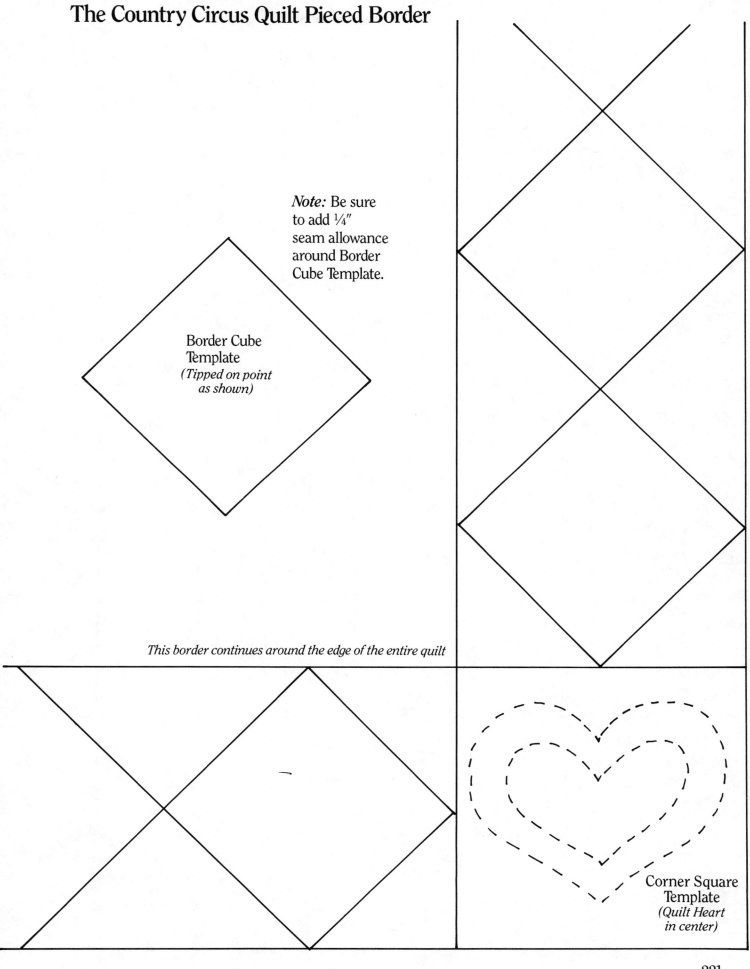

Note: Be sure to add ¼″ seam allowance around Border Cube Template.

Border Cube Template
(Tipped on point as shown)

This border continues around the edge of the entire quilt

Corner Square Template
(Quilt Heart in center)

Yardage for Applique for
Noah's Country Ark Quilt

1⅜ yard—*Light Blue*—Background diamond
2¾ yard—*Beige*—Background diamond
Rainbow Colors:
    Yellow—*¾ yard* (This is also enough for sun, pieced rays, bird beaks and legs)
    Poppy Red—*1⅛ yard* (This is also enough for binding)
    Raspberry—*⅜ yard*
    Blue—*⅜ yard*
Pieced Rays—*⅛ yard each* of 3 yellow/gold fabrics; the fourth yellow is included in yardage of Rainbow.
    ⅛ yard each of 5 blue/green fabrics
¼ yard—*Solid dark brown*—Ark
½ yard—*Solid medium brown*—Monkey heads, Camel Ⓑ body
⅛ yard—*Dark brown print*—Ram and Sheep heads, feet
½ yard—*Brown print*—Ark, Camel Ⓐ body
½ yard—*Brown print*—Monkey upper arm, Monkey body
½ yard—*Brown print*—Ark, Porcupine, Lion body
¼ yard—*Rust/brown print*—Giraffe accent spots, Ark windows
⅛ yard—*Striped brown print*—Porcupine accents
⅛ yard—*Light brown print*—Camel Ⓐ head
½ yard—*Tan print*—Lioness body, Lion mane
⅛ yard—*Tan print*—Lioness head, Lion head, Camel Ⓑ head
⅛ yard—*Tan print*—Monkey leg/tail
¼ yard—*Tan print*—Sheep body, Dove front wing
¾ yard—*Solid gold*—Lion mane, Lion tail tip, Giraffe bodies
1 yard—*Solid medium gray*—Zebra manes, Tail tip, Elephant heads, Shy hippo head, Raccoon feet, Porcupine head
½ yard—*Solid dark gray*—Raccoon bodies (note: should be very dark to contrast against elephant bodies), Porcupine feet
½ yard—*Medium gray print*—Elephant body, Penguin body
½ yard—*Dark gray print*—Shy hippo body
½ yard—*Light gray print*—Elephant body, Open-mouth hippo
⅛ yard—*Light gray print*—Raccoon tail accents
¾ yard—*Black print*—Raccoon mask (note: eyes on mask should either be lighter or darker for contrast), Raccoon paw pads, Tropical bird bodies, Ark Roof, Ark inner windows, Peacock body
½ yard—*Black print*—Zebra stripes, Penguin body, Open-mouth hippo throat
1 yard—*Off-White print (white on white)*—Zebra bodies, Zebra heads, Ram body, Ark, Dove Body, Dove back wing
¼ yard—*Bright White print*—Elephant tusks, Penguin body accents, Hippo teeth
¼ yard—*Solid purple*—Peacock feather fan
⅛ yard—*Solid magenta*—Peacock feather accent, Open-mouth hippo tongue
⅛ yard—*Solid aqua*—Peacock feather accent tip
⅛ yard—*Solid pink*—Elephants inner ears, Open-mouth hippo tonsils
⅛ yard—*Solid flesh*—Lion and Lioness noses, Zebra noses, Monkey noses
¼ yard—*Green print*
¼ yard—*Green print*
¼ yard—*Green print* } *5 Different fabrics create*
¼ yard—*Dark green print* *the entire "Hill".*
¼ yard—*Light green print*
½ yard—*Solid green*—Leaves
½ yard—*Green print*—Leaves
2 yards—Quilt Backing
1 package Green Bias Tape—for winding Vine

Yardage for Applique for
The Country Circus Quilt

1½ yard—*Off-white*—Background
1 yard—*Lavender print*—Triangles
½ yard—*Turquoise*—Pieced fan
⅓ yard—*Pale lavender*—Pieced fan
¼ yard—*Amethyst*—Seal, Wagon roof
1/16 yard—*Peach*—Seal platform, Hearts on wheels
¼ yard—*Dark purple*—Elephant bodies, Ball, Seal flipper
¼ yard—*Light purple*—Elephant heads
1 yard—*Lavender*—Pieced Border, Seal platform, Wagon wheels, Elephant toes and inner ears
1⅛ yard—*Blue*—Pieced Border (also includes binding)
¼ yard—*Light blue*—Pieced Corner Squares, Ball, Wagon Roof Hearts, Large Wagon Scallop
¼ yard—*Gold*—Wagon scallops, Giraffe bodies
¼ yard—*Orange*—Wagon bars, Elephant blankets, Giraffe spots, Ball, Elephant hats
1/16 yard—*White*—Elephant tusks
1¾ yard—Quilt Backing

The fabrics listed are to create the original colors used in the Noah's Country Ark Quilt and The Country Circus Quilt. These are only suggestions! The possibilities are endless! Use your imagination and be creative!

The People's Place Quilt Museum

About The Old Country Store

Cheryl A. Benner and Rachel T. Pellman are on the staff of The Old Country Store, located along Route 340 in Intercourse, Pennsylvania. The Store offers crafts from more than 300 artisans, most of whom are local Amish and Mennonites. There are quilts of traditional and contemporary designs, patchwork pillows and pillow kits, afghans, stuffed animals, dolls, tablecloths and Christmas tree ornaments. Other handcrafted items include potholders, sunbonnets and wooden toys.

For the do-it-yourself quilter, the Store offers quilt supplies, fabric at discount prices, and a large selection of quilt books and patterns.

Located on the second floor of the Store is The People's Place Quilt Museum. The Museum, which opened in 1988, features antique Amish quilts and crib quilts, as well as a small collection of dolls, doll quilts, socks and other decorative arts.

Cheryl Benner holding Austin Benner, Jesse Pellman, Rachel T. Pellman and Nathaniel Pellman.

About the Authors

Cheryl A. Benner and Rachel T. Pellman together developed the book **Country Quilts for Children.** Benner created the patterns, then selected fabrics, together they supervised the making of the original quilts by Lancaster County Mennonite women. This is Benner's and Pellman's sixth collaboration on quilt designs with related books. Their earlier books are the popular *The Country Love Quilt, The Country Lily Quilt, The Country Songbird Quilt, The Country Bride Quilt Collection* and *The Country Paradise Quilt.*

Benner, her husband Lamar, and young son live in Honeybrook, Pa. She is a graduate of the Art Institute of Philadelphia (Pa.). Benner is art director for Good Enterprises, Intercourse, Pa.

Pellman lives near Lancaster, Pa., and is manager of The Old Country Store, Intercourse. She is co-author of *The Country Bride Quilt.* She is also the author of *Amish Quilt Patterns* and *Small Amish Quilt Patterns;* co-author with Jan Steffy of *Patterns for Making Amish Dolls and Doll Clothes;* and co-author with her husband, Kenneth, of *A Treasury of Amish Quilts, The World of Amish Quilts, Amish Crib Quilts,* and *Amish Doll Quilts, Dolls and Other Playthings.*

The Pellmans are the parents of two sons.